ALGONQUIANS
OF THE EAST COAST
✠

This volume is one of a series that chronicles the history and culture of the Native Americans. Other books in the series include:

THE FIRST AMERICANS
THE SPIRIT WORLD
THE EUROPEAN CHALLENGE
PEOPLE OF THE DESERT
THE WAY OF THE WARRIOR
THE BUFFALO HUNTERS
REALM OF THE IROQUOIS
THE MIGHTY CHIEFTAINS
KEEPERS OF THE TOTEM
CYCLES OF LIFE

WAR FOR THE PLAINS
TRIBES OF THE SOUTHERN WOODLANDS
THE INDIANS OF CALIFORNIA
PEOPLE OF THE ICE AND SNOW
PEOPLE OF THE LAKES
THE WOMAN'S WAY
INDIANS OF THE WESTERN RANGE
HUNTERS OF THE NORTHERN FOREST
TRIBES OF THE SOUTHERN PLAINS
THE RESERVATIONS

The Cover: Tattoos representing birds and a snake adorn the forehead of Lapowinsa, a Lenape chief, in a portrait painted by Swedish artist Gustavus Hesselius in 1735, shortly before the Lenape lost their last major reserve along the Delaware River to white settlers. The bulk of the tribe moved west and ended up in Oklahoma, where they are known today as the Delaware.

ALGONQUIANS
OF THE EAST COAST
✤

by
THE EDITORS
of
TIME-LIFE BOOKS

ALEXANDRIA, VIRGINIA

Time-Life Books is a division of Time Life Inc.

PRESIDENT and CEO: John M. Fahey Jr.

TIME-LIFE BOOKS

MANAGING EDITOR: Roberta Conlan

Director of Design: Michael Hentges
Editorial Production Manager: Ellen Robling
Senior Editors: Russell B. Adams Jr., Janet Cave,
Lee Hassig, Robert Somerville, Henry Woodhead
Special Projects Editor: Rita Thievon Mullin
Director of Operations: Eileen Bradley
Director of Photography and Research:
John Conrad Weiser
Library: Louise D. Forstall

PRESIDENT: John D. Hall

Vice President, Director of New Product Development:
Neil Kagan
Associate Director, New Product Development:
Elizabeth D. Ward
Marketing Director: Pamela R. Farrell
Vice President, Book Production: Marjann Caldwell
Production Manager: Marlene Zack
Quality Assurance Manager: Miriam P. Newton

Library of Congress Cataloging in Publication Data
Algonquians of the east coast/by the editors of
Time-Life Books.
    p. cm. — (The American Indians)
    Includes bibliographical references and index.
    ISBN 0-8094-9738-7
    1. Algonquian Indians—History. 2. Algonquian
Indians—Social life and customs. I. Time-Life
Books. II. Series.
E99.A35A46 1995   95-35037
974'.004973—dc20   CIP

THE AMERICAN INDIANS

SERIES EDITOR: Henry Woodhead
Administrative Editor: Loretta Y. Britten

Editorial Staff for *Algonquians of the East Coast*
Senior Art Director: Dale Pollekoff
Picture Editor: Jane Coughran
Text Editors: Steve Hyslop (principal),
Denise Dersin, John Newton
Associate Editor/Research-Writing:
Robert H. Wooldridge Jr.
Senior Copyeditor: Ann Lee Bruen
Picture Coordinator: Daryl Beard
Editorial Assistant: Christine Higgins

Special Contributors: Robert Kyle, Tom Lewis,
Susan Perry, Lydia Preston, David S. Thomson
(text); Maureen McHugh, Elizabeth Thompson
(research-writing); Martha Lee Beckington,
Ellen Gross-Gerth, Barbara L. Klein, Carla Reissman,
Anne Whittle (research); Julie Sherman Grayson
(index).

Correspondents: Gevene Hertz (Copenhagen),
Christine Hinze (London), Christina Lieberman
(New York). Valuable assistance was also provided
by: Elizabeth Brown (New York), John Dunne
(Australia).

R 10 9 8 7 6 5 4 3 2 1

CONTENTS

1
THE ORIGINAL PEOPLE
16

2
CONFRONTING THE COLONISTS
64

3
THE SEARCH FOR RESTITUTION
122

ESSAYS

CLOSE TO THE DAWNLAND
6
TOMAH JOSEPH'S BIRCH BARK STORIES
54
MICMAC QUILLWORK
105
SACRED SMOKE RISING
112
A FEAST FOR THE WAMPANOAG
160

ACKNOWLEDGMENTS 170
BIBLIOGRAPHY 170
PICTURE CREDITS 171
INDEX 172

CLOSE TO THE DAWNLAND

For Algonquians of the East Coast, the rising of the sun from the eastern waters over forests and mountains was a daily reminder of their wondrous emergence as a people. Some tribes traced their origins to a giant who came from the sea and freed the first humans from the trees that encased them. Others told of the Great Hare who sprang from the land of the rising sun and formed a bountiful world for people to inhabit. All along the coast, tribes gave thanks that they lay close to the Dawnland, or the bright beginning of things.

For untold generations, Algonquians fulfilled that promise by drawing sustenance from fields, forests, and waterways without exhausting their gifts. By the 1600s, however, strangers from beyond the sea were settling on

The towering grandeur of Mount Katahdin in northern Maine is reflected in the glistening surface of a nearby lake. The peak remains sacred to the Penobscot Indians and other Eastern Abenakis of the area, who refer to it as the Greatest Mountain and say that its spirit controls the weather.

the coast and vying for the land's rewards. In time, those intruders would claim ownership of the Indian domain.

In spite of that loss, many places sacred to the Algonquians would remain theirs in spirit, if not in title. Tribes endured in the area and affirmed through their legends and ceremonies that this was the land where their ancestors, the original people, first saw the light.

LAKE OF THE TRANSFORMER

WESTERN ABENAKI WOMEN, 1800s

The serene expanse of Lake Champlain forms the border between New York and Vermont. According to a legend of the Western Abenaki, the transformer Odzihoso molded himself from mere dust and set about shaping the earth to his liking. When his task was completed, he changed himself into an outcropping of rock in Lake Champlain so that he could forever overlook and admire his handiwork.

THE GIANT'S CLIFFS

Waves roll in from the Atlantic below the clay cliffs of Gay Head on the island of Martha's Vineyard, home to Wampanoags who migrated from the Massachusetts mainland. Wampanoag lore tells of a protective giant known as Maushop, sent here by the Creator to watch over the people. When the time came for the giant to depart, Wampanoags gathered at the cliffs and watched Maushop swim away in the guise of an immense whale.

WAMPANOAG EMMA M. STAFFORD IN 1923

THE LENAPE'S RIVERINE REALM

Water cascades through lush greenery on a tributary of the upper Delaware River, homeland of the Munsee branch of the Lenape, known to European colonists as the Delaware. In early times, Lenapes gathered annually for religious ceremonies on nearby Minisink Island.

LENAPE MOTHER AND
DAUGHTER, 1915

POWHATAN'S LUSH DOMAIN

The Pamunkey River flows past the Pamunkey Indian Reservation, located near land sacred to the followers of Powhatan, whose multitribal chiefdom covered much of Tidewater Virginia in the early 1600s. The leading Powhatan temple was located nearby, and according to tribal tradition, the chief himself was laid to rest in the area. His spirit, it was said, journeyed to the land of the rising sun, where souls are renewed.

PAMUNKEY MAN
IN CEREMONIAL
REGALIA, 1899

1

THE ORIGINAL PEOPLE

A formidable palisade of timbers protects an early Algonquian village visited in 1585 by artist John White, a member of the first English expedition to land on the coast of today's North Carolina. Like other Algonquians of the East Coast, the Roanoke Indians whom White encountered believed that the land was given to them by great spirits, and they were prepared to defend that inheritance.

On chill winter nights, when the snow lay deep against their bark-covered lodges, Algonquians of northern New England gathered about the fire and told tales of the mythic hero Gluskab, a giant who came from across the sea in a granite canoe. Some said that when Gluskab reached land long ago, there were no people there to greet him, so he drew his great bow and split open the ash trees, and the first humans stepped from the bark. Gluskab did all he could to make their world a more inviting place. To free the streams and rivers, he slew a froglike monster who was hoarding the waters in its swollen belly. To quiet the gusts that stirred up storm waves and bent the treetops, he captured the mighty Wind Eagle and bound it so tightly that a stifling calm descended. Recognizing his error, Gluskab loosened the Wind Eagle's wings, and cool breezes wafted across the land.

To give people plenty to feast on, Gluskab decided to fill the forest with animals. A towering figure himself, he made the first creatures so large that they dwarfed the humans. The Moose, for instance, stood as high as the tallest pine tree. Concerned for his people, Gluskab asked the Moose what he would do if he saw a man coming. The Moose vowed that he would bring trees crashing down on the intruder, so Gluskab made the animal smaller to ensure that he would be the one to fall when hunters came stalking. Next Gluskab asked the ferocious White Bear what he would do if he met with a man. "Eat him," replied the animal gruffly; so Gluskab sent him to live among the rocks and ice, where he could do people no harm. In this manner, Gluskab questioned all the animals and, after hearing their answers, changed their size or habitat accordingly. Thereafter, when creatures of the forest saw a man approaching, they turned and ran.

Gluskab taught people how to track and snare those skittish animals and where to find wild vegetables and herbs for food and medicine. He showed them how to build houses and canoes and kindle fires. He taught them the names of all the stars that blazed in the heavens. When he had made the world fit for humans, Gluskab left them and went to dwell in the depths of the forest with his grandmother. "I go away now," he said to the people, "but I shall return again. When you feel the ground tremble, then know it is I." In his absence, the people fell prey to misfortune, and strangers from distant lands trespassed on their domain. But Algonquians knew that Gluskab had not forgotten them. As one storyteller put it, "Wherever he might be in the wilderness, he was never very far from any of the Indians." Some day the earth would tremble, the elders said, and Gluskab would come back to reclaim his country and the creatures he cared for above all others.

As such legends attest, Algonquians of the East Coast regard themselves as the original people. Theirs is the land of the rising sun, and that bright sense of promise remains an important part of their identity. Algonquians of northern New England call themselves the Wabanaki, or People of the Dawnland. And the Ojibwa and other Algonquian-speaking groups living far inland around the Great Lakes say that they too are original people, or Anishinabe, whose ancestors once lived in the Dawnland, by the great salt sea, before prophets guided them westward.

Aside from such intriguing legends, the origins and early migrations of the Algonquians remain shrouded in mystery. By the time Europeans

Delicately crafted by a Passamaquoddy artisan, this birch-bark container, called a "makuk," is one of many useful objects fashioned by Algonquians of northern New England from the pliable bark of the paper birch tree that flourished in the cold climate.

The realm of the eastern Algonquians, stretching down the Atlantic coast from the Canadian Maritimes to the Carolina capes, comprised dozens of distinct tribal homelands. The larger groups are identified in their territories here, along with the major rivers that linked tribes of the interior to the coast and its abundant resources.

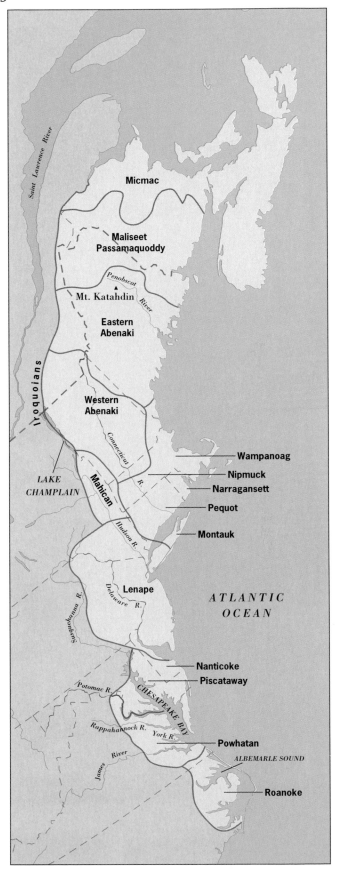

made contact with them, however, they had fanned out across a vast area of North America. A few Algonquian groups ventured onto the Plains—among them the Blackfeet, Cheyenne, and Arapaho. But most adhered to the woodlands, where they divided into two kindred language groups: the central Algonquians, residing in the heart of Canada and around the western Great Lakes; and the eastern Algonquians, living along the Atlantic coast from the Gulf of Saint Lawrence to the tidewater of North Carolina. Between the two lay the realm of the Iroquois and other members of the Iroquoian language family, extending from the mouth of the Saint Lawrence River to Lake Erie.

Despite wide variations in speech between the eastern and central Algonquians, they retained certain stories and rituals in common. Indians from Manitoba to Maine warned of a cannibal monster who came down from the north to devour people and believed that it was proper to tell sacred stories only in winter, when snakes and menacing underwater spirits were safely hidden beneath the snow and ice. And tribal groups living as far apart as the shores of Lake Superior and the tidal inlets of Chesapeake Bay told of a fabled creature called the Great Hare, who dwelt in the land of the rising sun and played a part in the miracle of creation.

Although the various Algonquian tribes of the East Coast shared in this cultural inheritance, they pursued ways of life that differed significantly from north to south. At the northern end of the coastal region, the climate was cold, the terrain rugged, and the growing season brief. The tribal groups there, known collectively as the Wabanaki, all relied heavily on hunting, fishing, and gathering. The Micmac of present-day New Brunswick cultivated no crops other than tobacco, while groups residing in or around Maine, New Hampshire, and Vermont—including the Maliseet and Passamaquoddy and the Eastern and Western Abenaki—reaped limited harvests of corn and other crops, mostly in fertile river valleys like the Merrimack and the upper Connecticut. As

A 19th-century painting depicts Micmacs of Canada at home and on the hunt. Women in French-inspired peaked bonnets help with the paddling, as men hunt fowl from birch-bark canoes, one of which carries a small sail. Inside the bark-covered lodge in the background, a woman sits with a cradleboard on her lap and several birch-bark containers at her feet.

if to compensate the northerners for the rigors of their environment, Nature blessed them with gifts that were rare or nonexistent to the south, including the moose—a source of meat, hide, and fur—and the paper birch tree, whose bark could be crafted into durable lightweight containers and canoes. These Algonquians had a busy seasonal round, marked by frequent moves from camp to camp in pursuit of wild resources. Often they traveled by water, paddling their canoes along clear-flowing rivers and crystal-blue lakes.

In southern New England, the climate and soil allowed for substantial harvests, but people still shifted base during the course of the year to make the most of diverse resources. Many tribal bands dispersed each summer in small family groups to cultivate gardens near the coast, then reconvened at larger winter villages that lay inland, in sheltered pockets of the forest where hunters did not have to venture too far to find quarry. This pattern prevailed among such groups as the Nipmuck, Massachusett, and Wampanoag of Massachusetts; the Narragansett of Rhode Island; and the Mohegan and Pequot of Connecticut.

In the Middle Atlantic region, from the Hudson River valley southward, the growing conditions were even better, and many groups lived near their gardens for much of the year. The Mahican of the upper Hudson River valley, for example, lived in clusters of longhouses close to their cornfields from early spring to late fall, when they fanned out in small groups to winter hunting camps. Many Lenapes along the lower Hudson and along the Delaware River and its tributaries lived in a similar manner. The name Lenape, like that of many Native American groups, meant "people." In the proud manner of Algonquians elsewhere, they sometimes referred to themselves as Lenni-Lenape, or "original people." But English colonists dubbed them the Delaware—a title they themselves embraced when pressure from white settlers forced them to migrate far from their beloved homeland.

At the southern end of the Algonquian domain, around Chesapeake Bay and Albemarle Sound, villagers profited from a growing season that lasted more than five months and a broad coastal plain, laced with tidal waterways and laden with rich deposits of silt. The fine opportunities here for farming, combined with an abundance of fish, game, and other forage, made this an especially rewarding environment. Among the groups who flourished here were the Roanoke of North Carolina, the Piscataway and Nanticoke of Maryland, and Virginia's Powhatan—a name that referred originally to a single tribe along the James River and its ambitious chief. By the time English colonists reached the area in the early 1600s, Chief Powhatan had claimed authority over some 30 tribes, known collectively by his name. Amid their bounty, the Powhatan and their southern Algonquian neighbors evolved a complex social structure, with marked disparities in wealth and status between the leaders and their followers.

One common thread in the diverse subsistence patterns of the eastern Algonquians was their reliance on the coastal water-ways. Even groups who lived well inland derived plenty from the sea each spring when herring, shad, smelt, sturgeon, salmon, and other saltwater fish thronged upstream to spawn in fresh water. Among the best places to catch them were near falls or rapids, where the rivers narrowed and the fish became bottled up. Larger species were speared or netted, and smaller ones were snared in basket weirs or other traps. From the Roanoke River in the south to the Saint John River in the north—and along scores of inlets in between—Algonquians convened annually at the spawning grounds to partake of this generous offering, which brought them plenty at the leanest time of the year.

According to a legend of the Mashpee, a Wampanoag group native to Cape Cod, the spawning runs in their country were inspired by the songs of Ahsoo, a homely young woman with a beautiful voice. "Her chin was point-ed and sharp as the beak of a loon, her nose was humped and crooked, and her eyes were as big as a frightened deer's," the tale relates, but "no woman could equal her in singing. Birds paused on the bough to listen to her, and the river, running over rapids, almost ceased its flowing to hear." So entic-ing were her songs that the "river at the foot of the hill became alive with fishes, journeying up from the South Sea to hear the voice of Ahsoo." One of those lured by her singing was the Trout Chief, a monster of a fish who forged his own path inland from the sea, known today as Cotuit Brook. He labored so hard to reach Ahsoo that he died at the end of his journey.

Up and down the Atlantic coast, Algonquians marked time by the spawning runs. The Penobscot—a band of Eastern Abenakis living along Maine's Penobscot River—called April the Spearfish Moon, or the Month of Smelts. During the same season, Mahicans along the Hudson River, Lenapes along the Delaware, and Powhatans along the James River and nearby waterways were taking vast quantities of herring and shad. Those few groups who did not join in the harvest themselves sometimes bartered with coastal tribes for dried fish.

Other maritime resources were available to Algonquians throughout the year, including oysters, clams, and other shellfish, whose meat could

An Abenaki demonstrates the time-honored technique of snaring fish with a long-handled spear, whose traditional wooden or bone prongs were replaced after European contact with metal ones, as on the 19th-century example at near right. Such weapons were useful in any season, but Abenakis made the most of them in April, or the Spearfish Moon, when salmon, sturgeon, and other species made their spawning runs.

also be preserved and transported inland. Huge shell heaps, representing hundreds of years of harvesting by Indians, have been identified along shores from Maine to North Carolina. Tribes throughout the region sought shells from the coast, including treasured strings of wampum, which played an important part in ceremonies and later served in some places as a form of currency. Among the leading producers of wampum were the Shinnecock and the Montauk bordering Long Island Sound, whose shores abounded in white whelk shells and purple quahog shells that the wampum makers pierced with drills of stone and strung in intricate patterns.

The sea and the rivers that flowed into it offered many other gifts to the Algonquians. Micmacs and other northern peoples sometimes disguised themselves in animal skins and stalked seals that were sleeping along the rocky shore, killing them with clubs or harpoons. Occasionally hunters on the New England coast ventured out into bays or coves in pursuit of porpoises or stray whales. When a whale washed ashore, an entire

Never far from a river, bay, or estuary, the eastern Algonquians developed sundry gear for catching fish, including nets of hemp or other fiber, stitched together with wooden needles; hooks of carved bone; and basket traps of intertwined reeds or twigs.

WAMPANOAG LOBSTER NET

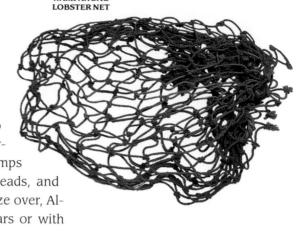

village or group of families would gather on the beach to butcher the animal and make use of its meat, oil, and bone. Farther inland, people groped through the muddy bottoms of swamps and slow-moving rivers and pulled out horned pout, bullheads, and plump, sweet-tasting eels. In the winter, when the waters froze over, Algonquians fished through the ice with long deer-bone spears or with lines made of twisted hemp or other fiber and fitted with small bone hooks. William Wood, a colonist in the Massachusetts Bay area, observed in the 1630s that Indians there were "experienced in the knowledge of all

PAMUNKEY NETTING NEEDLE

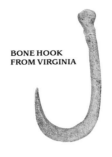

**BONE HOOK
FROM VIRGINIA**

Holding a long spear, Tom Hill of the Poos-patuck—a small tribe on the south shore of Long Island—fishes the shallows of a bay in a picture taken in the early 1900s. Behind Hill stands a large rack used for drying nets; to his right is a basket made of iron strips that Poospatucks filled with hay and set alight to provide a torch for night fishing.

baits, and diverse seasons . . . knowing when to fish in rivers, and when at rocks, when in bays, and when at seas."

The region's myriad waterways were not only important sources of nourishment but also vital lines of communication. Most settlements were located along rivers, streams, or lakes, and Algonquians traveled by water whenever possible, whether for seasonal migrations, for warfare, or for trade. Although people sometimes bartered for food or hides, most groups met their own basic needs and traded mainly for exotic items that dazzled the eye or soothed the spirit. During the summer months, Algonquian traders went from village to village, bearing leather pouches stuffed with a variety of items not widely available, from the yaupon holly—a medicinal plant valued as a ceremonial purge—to pearls pried from oysters or freshwater mussels. Flint, copper, and brightly colored feathers were also popular trading items, as were pigments, including a powdered red root that the Powhatan called *puccoon* and mixed with oil or grease to paint their bodies.

In the southern and central regions, Algonquians traveled in dugout canoes made from logs of cypress, cedar, or elm, but in northern New England, people favored birch-bark canoes, which were less durable and easier to capsize but lighter, faster, and far more portable. Dugout canoes tended to be too heavy to portage from one body of water to another. Travelers had to hide them along the shore and hope that the canoes would still be there on their return trip. To help camouflage a dugout, canoe makers would sometimes leave the bark of the tree on the boat's underside so that it looked like a fallen log when overturned.

When traveling by foot, Algonquians followed ancient, well-worn trails that ran parallel to rivers and lakes or connected one valley or estuary to the next. The Powhatan and other tightly knit tribal groups had paths linking all their villages, some of which were part of larger trails that continued on to neighboring territories. Long-distance trade was frequently conducted in many stages, with traders receiving and passing along items from far-off places they had never visited.

Traders and other travelers passing through the territory of friendly tribes were greeted with great courtesy. Upon reaching a village, they

**NANTICOKE
BASKET TRAP**

were often feasted by the local chief. Guests of the Powhatan entered the chief's house by passing through a friendly gantlet of villagers, who saluted them with shouts. The Lenape considered it impolite to ask any questions of visitors before serving them food and drink. Although a pipe of tobacco might be shared with newcomers, any important business was deferred until the next day, after the guests had had an opportunity to rest. Lenape travelers expected similar hospitality when they ventured far from home, and any chief who failed to welcome them properly risked being regarded as an enemy in the future.

Women often accompanied men on trading missions. When traveling by water, they paddled along with the men. When trekking overland, they carried most of the provisions—not because they were considered their husbands' servants but because the men needed to have their hands free to wield weapons should animals or enemies appear suddenly on the trail.

When friendly parties met on a trail, they usually stopped and sat down together under a tree to smoke tobacco, exchange news, and per- haps share a meal. Most Algonquians traveled light. Wampanoag men, for example, often journeyed for days carrying only a bow, a quiver of arrows, a pipe, several flints, and small amounts of parched cornmeal and tobacco packed in pouches hanging from the waist or neck. Trained for endurance running from early childhood, Wampanoag men could travel with such a load at a jogging pace for much of the day with relative ease.

Even in unfamiliar territory, Algonquians seldom lost their way. "They are expert travelers," commented John Lawson, a young Englishman who canoed with Indians for more than 500 miles in the Carolinas in 1701. "They will find the head of any river, though it is five, six or seven hundred miles off, and they never were there in their lives before; as is often proved, by their appointing to meet on the head of such a river, where perhaps none of them ever was before, but where they shall rendezvous exactly at the prefixt time." Lenapes prided themselves on returning from a lengthy trip at precisely the date they had set with their relatives before leaving. Among some tribes, villagers sent out search parties immediately if a group failed to appear on the appointed day.

Travelers often carved marks of various kinds into trees along the trails, sometimes to give assurance to fellow tribesmen that they were on the right path and sometimes to pass on news of recent run-ins with enemies. To mark an event of historical significance, Wampanoags dug holes about a foot deep and a foot wide along the side of the trails that crisscrossed their lands. Thereafter, each time a group of Wampanoags

Graceful birch-bark canoes, some of them propped on logs for repairs, line a beach near Bar Harbor on Maine's rocky coast in a 1910 photograph of a village of the Penobscot, a branch of the Eastern Abenaki. The Penobscot have been masters of canoe building since ancient times.

passed one of the holes, they cleared it of debris and retold the story it commemorated, thus preserving a record for future generations.

Algonquians knew the forests as well as they did the waterways. From the limbs of alder or hazel trees they fashioned arrows, from ash and beech trees bows and snowshoes, and from hickory trees tool handles. Tribes in some areas carved the broad, straight trunk of the white elm into dugout canoes and used its inner bark for fishnets and medicine. The gum of balsam firs served as a sealant, and the pitch of pine trees as fuel for torches. The roots of the red cedar were plied into a heavy-duty thread, used to stitch together basswood-bark mats for the roofing and walls of homes.

Trees also provided sustenance. Walnuts, hickory nuts, beechnuts, butternuts, and chestnuts could be eaten raw, or dried and pounded into

flour, with which the Algonquians made breads and thickened stews. Various tribes used walnuts to make a kind of baby formula, mixing the ground nuts with cornmeal and water to form a thin sweet liquid that infants relished. Elizabeth Hanson, a New Hampshire settler who was captured by a French and Indian war party in 1724, told how her baby was saved when an Indian woman taught her how to make the liquid when she found herself unable to produce any more breast milk. Her infant, she wrote, "quickly began to thrive and look well, which gave me great comfort." Farther south, the Powhatan considered walnut milk a delicacy and served it to honored guests. In many places, people filled out their diet by eating the fibrous inner bark of conifers. The Iroquois referred to Algonquians of the Hudson River region as Adirondack, or "bark eaters."

The great trees of the eastern forests provided further nourishment during the spring, when women collected sap from a number of trees, among them birch, hickory, and ash. Here as in the Great Lakes region, however, the sap of the sugar maple was especially prized for its sweetness. Native New Englanders collected it in birch-bark containers and boiled it down into syrup and sugar. In Maine, Eastern Abenakis made a wholesome meal by mixing syrup with wild artichokes and groundnuts. They also melted pieces of sugar in water, which they then drank for nourishment. Pehr Kalm, a Swede traveling among tribes of the East Coast

Using an age-old Algonquian device, a veteran Penobscot hunter first mimics the cry of a female moose by blowing through a cone of rolled birch bark (above, left), then dips the instrument in the lake and lets the water trickle out to imitate the sound of the female moose drinking or urinating. Attracted by the noises, bull moose would emerge from the forest onto the shore, giving hunters a clear shot at their prey, depicted at right on a quill-decorated moose caller of Micmac design.

in the 1700s, told of having "many good meals of just sugar and bread when no other food was available."

From ponds, marshes, and grassy clearings, Algonquians gathered a host of wild plants, including edible tubers such as the sweet, sticky root of the yellow pond lily, which they boiled and roasted. To Europeans, it tasted like sheep's liver. Indians around Chesapeake Bay derived great nourishment from the starchy roots called tuckahoe, which flourished in freshwater marshes. People all along the coast ate the tender spring greens of plants like the marsh marigold and fiddle fern and flavored their stews with wild leeks, milkweed flowers, rose hips, and other herbs and seeds. Western Abenakis around Lake Champlain had many uses for the humble cattail. They ate the young plant's shoots in the spring and its small flowers and seeds in the summer and fall. They dried and pounded the mature plant into flour or boiled it to make syrup. Abenaki women padded their babies' bedding and dressed their children's burns with the cattail's soft down. And men used the plant's sturdy stems to make darts.

Berries grew along the coast in astonishing variety and profusion, not only in natural clearings but also in fields that had been farmed out and left fallow. Thimbleberries, raspberries, blackberries, elderberries, shadberries, blueberries, cranberries, and currants—all were part of the Algonquian diet. "The berry is the wonder of all the fruits growing naturally in these parts," wrote Roger Williams, the Englishman who founded the colony of Rhode Island. "In some parts where the natives have planted, I have many times seen as many as would fill a good ship within a few miles compass." The most popular of the edible berries was the wild strawberry, which the New England Algonquians called grassberry and those who dwelt farther south gave the lyrical name of heartberry.

From the rich and varied plant life around them, the Algonquians evolved an impressive pharmacopoeia. Early European visitors to the coast often remarked that Indian

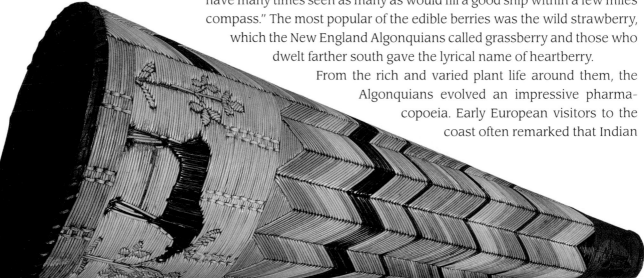

medicines proved to be more effective than their own. Algonquian healers used hundreds of plants and their extracts to treat minor maladies as well as grave ills. A gargle made from wild blackberry root, for example, helped soothe a sore throat. A decoction made from unripe cranberries helped draw out the venom from a poisoned arrow.

Snug bark-covered wigwams like this replica at Waterloo Village in northwestern New Jersey kept Lenape hunters warm and dry in their winter camps. Many Algonquians took shelter in similar structures when they ventured out during the winter to pursue deer, moose, and other sources of meat and fur.

In order to cure diarrhea, Penobscots drank a tea from boiled white-oak bark. To reduce fevers, Lenapes sipped an infusion made from dog-wood bark. To heal wounds, Micmacs applied a salve made from the berries of the spikenard, a member of the ginseng family.

The great woods in which the coastal Algonquians dwelt also provided them with plenty of game animals, including deer, elk, raccoon, bear, fox, otter, rabbit, mink, porcupine, and, in the northern regions, moose. Numerous game birds could be found in or near the woods as well, including partridge, woodcock, quail, turkey, and swarms of the now extinct passenger pigeon. Both fresh- and saltwater marshes hosted immense flocks of migratory geese and ducks. For the Lenape and tribes to their south, the white-tailed deer was of special importance. Algonquians used its flesh for food, its hide for clothing, its hoofs for glue, its antlers and bone for tools, its sinew and gut for cord, and its suet for cooking. For Micmacs, the moose served a similar role, supplying them with much of their food and clothing.

The Algonquians wasted no part of a slain animal. They used deer brains, for example, to soften hides and employed tiny mink, raccoon, and otter bones—some with natural eyelets—as sewing needles. Beaver teeth became the sharp edges of hand tools, and beaver tail, often cooked in bear grease, was served at feasts up and down the Atlantic coast. Micmacs sometimes ate bear grease alone, as a snack. To keep it sweet, they stored it with sassafras or slippery-elm bark in animal bladders.

Every useful creature in nature—and all the tools hunters relied on to catch their prey—were seen as gifts from supreme powers to the original people. According to legend, Gluskab first summoned the Moose by taking a "strip of birch bark three hands long," rolling it into a horn, and using the instrument to lure the animal. After seizing the creature by the antlers and shrinking him down to size, Gluskab taught people how to snare the Moose: "To this day, the hunter calls him with a horn of birch bark."

Like Indians elsewhere, the Algonquians living along the Atlantic coast identified the passing months and seasons by changes in their surroundings or subsistence activities. For Micmacs, each month, or moon, was associated with the pursuit of one wild resource or another. January was a time for seal hunting, while March marked the beginning of the smelt runs, and April saw the return of geese from the south. September was a month for eel gathering or moose calling, depending on one's location, while October was the time to hunt fat elk and plump beaver. At the end of the year, Micmacs went out under the Tomcod Moon, as they called it, and fished for that cold-water species as it ran beneath the ice.

A Penobscot father and son set out on a winter hunting trip in Maine, the father carrying bow and arrows and a basswood bag, and his son equipped with a rifle and a basket pack woven of strips of ash. Both wear tapered, lightweight snowshoes of ash that helped hunters make speed as they tracked game through heavy snow.

Elsewhere, the seasonal round included farming as well as hunting and fishing. For Abenakis, May was the Planting Moon, a time to clear fields with stone hoes and sow corn, beans, and squash. Like most eastern Algonquians, Abenakis also grew tobacco, which they smoked on both social and ceremonial occasions. In the fall, when the maple leaves turned a brilliant red—after soaking up the blood that spilled from the night sky when the Great Bear expired, according to tribal legend—Abenakis harvested their crops, storing any surplus in underground cellars lined with birch bark. Those stores were seldom sufficient to last until spring, and Abenakis dispersed from their summer villages to camp and hunt in small bands through the winter, stalking deer and moose. Among the tribes of southern New England, in contrast, fall was a time for groups who had scattered in the spring to come back together at snug winter villages in the forest, from which hunters made forays when provisions ran short.

Farther south, among the Nanticoke and Powhatan, people lived in one place for most of the year, except for fishing and foraging expeditions in the spring and early summer and late-fall forays to hunting camps, where villagers remained for a month or so and took part in deer drives. The meat they preserved and the vegetables they stored saw them through the winter. Corn was so important to the Algonquians around Chesapeake Bay that they called the season between early summer and fall Nepinough, or Earing of the Corn. Corn alone accounted for up to half their diet. Here as elsewhere, Indians feasted on green corn and preserved the rest in the form of dried kernels, which women processed as needed by pounding them in wooden mortars and sifting out the chaff. When the geese returned from the north in the fall and the seasonal round began anew, most people in the southern region could look forward to another year without displacement or deprivation, barring drought or some other misfortune.

The shelters of the coastal Algonquians were nearly as diverse as their subsistence patterns. Although lodges in many parts of the region were referred to by an Algonquian term, *wigwam,* those built by Micmacs and some of their northern neighbors were shaped like tipis, with straight poles that interlocked at the top and a covering of bark. More typical of the region as a whole were loaf-shaped structures framed of bent sapling poles and covered with bark, hide, or reed mats. In the event of a move, sometimes the entire lodge was taken down and reconstructed elsewhere; in other cases, the framework remained in place, and the covering was carried from site to site. Well-built shelters like those villagers of the Chesapeake region occupied year-round were quite cozy in winter. Covered with

Wearing full ceremonial regalia, Chief Wise Owl of the Nipmuck of central Massachusetts cradles a tomato seedling in his palm during a spring ceremony called Seaquankeyquash, celebrating nature's emergence from the pall of winter. "On January 1, everything is cold and dead," Chief Wise Owl recited during the ceremony, "but in May the trees bud and grass grows and everything is new."

bark or tightly woven mats, they retained heat from the fire that flickered beneath the central smoke hole. On hot summer days, the walls could be lifted to permit air to circulate. Around the fire, platforms covered with mats or furs served as beds. Baskets brimming with bowls, ladles, medicines, sewing needles, and other household goods hung from the rafters.

Most dwellings in the region housed a single extended family, but some were larger and sheltered several related families. Some Abenakis and many Lenapes and Mahicans lived for much or part of the year in longhouses like those of the Iroquois. Sturdy, barrel-roofed structures about 20 feet wide and up to 100 or more feet long, they were sometimes partitioned into separate compartments for each family. A French missionary who stayed in an Abenaki longhouse in Maine during the early 1600s described the dwelling as "long and covered with the bark of trees of all kinds. The top is domed, with a hole over each fire to let out the smoke." Every family had its own hearth, he added, and some longhouses had as many as eight fires and housed up to 60 people. Raised sleeping platforms ran along the inside walls.

The preferred location for Algonquian villages was on high ground close to a river or lake whose banks offered good alluvial soil for farming

Nanticokes in Maryland use mortars made of hollowed logs to shell and grind corn, long the mainstay of Algonquians around Chesapeake Bay. The woman uses a pestle in a narrow grinding mortar to mash kernels that have been separated from the ears in the broad shelling mortar next to hers. Such shelling mortars had a row of sticks near the bottom spaced so that the loose kernels fell through to the opening at the base. Also used to separate kernels were handy wooden corn scrapers like the one pictured at right.

CORN SCRAPER

SHELLING MORTAR

and whose waters served both as a source of sustenance and as a means of travel. In general, settlements were smaller in the north and larger in the south, where some villages had as many as 100 lodges, each one sheltering six or more people. A number of villages along the East Coast were fortified with log palisades to protect against attack by rival Algonquians or by far-ranging Iroquois. Some groups erected palisades in remote spots and took shelter there only in times of peril. Throughout the region, most villages had sweat lodges and birthing and menstrual huts. Southern Algonquian villages often had other special structures as well, including storage sheds, temples, and a chief's lodge or council house—a large building decorated with spirit masks and icons where people gathered for celebrations and councils. To protect their crops, southern Algonquians also built a field watcher's hut, a raised shelter occupied by a sentinel who killed pests or shooed them away.

Algonquians used fire in various ways to mold their environment. Some groups burned over meadows and other choice hunting grounds annually to promote fresh growth that attracted deer and other browsing animals. To ease the task of clearing forested areas for planting, men often kindled small fires around the trunks of trees to kill them. The entire field was later set afire to burn the dead trees down to stumps and clear away the underbrush—a procedure that had the added benefit of coating the soil with nutrient-rich ash. To Europeans, the charred stumps that peppered the fields appeared untidy, but Algonquians simply planted seeds between them with their digging sticks. Once a field was in use, villagers in some places continued to burn it each year after the harvest to kill weeds and lay down a fresh layer of ash. Such techniques, combined with the practice of letting tired fields go fallow for a while before recultivating them, prolonged the life of a settlement.

Some seasonal tasks undertaken by Indians involved the joint effort of entire communities and took on a festive air. Roger Williams noted that when the Narragansett had a large chore to perform, such as breaking up a field for planting, they had a "very loving sociable speedy way to dispatch it: All the neighbors, men and women, 40, 50, 100, etc., join and come in to help freely. With

A plump duck roasts on a spit at a replica of a Piscataway village in Saint Marys City, Maryland. Closely related culturally to the Nanticoke of the Eastern Shore, the Piscataway lived west of Chesapeake Bay. Among the many foods they feasted on were oysters (below), rabbits and fish (bottom), and a cornucopia of vegetables and legumes (right), shown here in clay bowls of the sort Piscataways traditionally crafted.

friendly joining they break up their fields, build their forts, hunt the woods, stop and kill fish in the rivers."

When men and women worked together in the same basic activity, they often performed different functions. During group hunting expeditions, men stalked the animals, while women cleaned the hides and dried or smoked the meat. During the growing season, men often helped women prepare the fields, but women planted and tended all crops with the exception of tobacco, which men usually cultivated as a ceremonial responsibility.

Women also performed the housework, preparing food, tanning hides and tailoring them into clothing, as well as crafting mats, baskets, clay pots, and other household goods. With the help of their children, they gathered and stacked firewood, fetched water, and foraged widely from forest to seashore, picking berries one day and digging for clams the next. When it came time to move to a new camp, women dismantled and packed up the lodge, or its coverings, and reassembled it at the next location. Through it all, women reared the young, carrying their tightly swaddled infants around on straight, thin cradleboards, which mothers wore on their back or set safely nearby as they worked.

Algonquian men had fewer but equally demanding jobs. Aside from clearing fields, they were responsible for hunting, fishing, and making war, all strenuous and potentially dangerous tasks. A deer hunt might require a

This shapely wooden bowl was carved of elm burl about 1650 by Nipmucks or Mohegans of southern New England.

man to run for 20 miles or more in a single day. In between these expeditions, the men spent much of their time making and repairing their tools and weapons, including canoes. Powhatans created long dugout canoes that could carry up to 30 people by felling cedar logs, burning the wood repeatedly to hollow it, then carving and shaping it with stone hatchets and knives—a process that could take more than three weeks, even when women and children lent a hand, as they often did. Men also helped raise their sons by instructing them in such lore as imitating animal calls to lure prey or shooting at targets with toy bows. Sometimes, noted Roger Williams, a man would assist his mate with her chores, "either out of love for his wife or care for his children," but usually men and women kept to their own basic roles and responsibilities.

In the opinion of early Europeans, who considered hunting and fishing pleasant sport rather than hard work, the division of labor between Algonquian men and women seemed anything but equal. "The men employ their time wholly in hunting and other exercises of the bow," wrote Governor Edward Winslow of Plymouth in the early 1600s, "except that they sometimes take some pains at fishing. The women live a most slavish life: They carry all their burdens, set and dress their corn, gather it in, and seek out for much of their food, beat and make ready the corn to eat, and have all household care lying upon them."

What Winslow and other early observers failed to appreciate, however, was that the labor women performed, particularly in the fields, brought them great credit. Here as in other regions where tribes relied significantly on farming, women were valued all the more for that vital contribution. Indeed, everything Algonquian women produced was theirs to dispose of—the household stores of

The clay pot below with its graceful flaring collar, crafted by a Wampanoag artisan near Cape Cod about 1620, was made not only to be used but also to be admired.

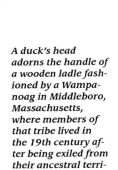

A duck's head adorns the handle of a wooden ladle fashioned by a Wampanoag in Middleboro, Massachusetts, where members of that tribe lived in the 19th century after being exiled from their ancestral territory near Plymouth.

corn, the clay pots, the woven baskets and mats, the hides they fashioned into clothing. If a couple separated, the woman retained those assets—and usually the house and children as well. Among the Lenape, a man lived with his wife's family. Should they separate—a decision more likely to be made by the wife than the husband—his wife piled his few personal possessions outside the lodge, and he returned to the house of his mother or other close female relative. Among some groups, including the Narragansett and the Powhatan, a woman might succeed her husband or brother as chief.

Whatever distinctions a particular tribe made between men and women when it came to matters of property or lineage, most Algonquian marriages were equitable. Divorce was rare, and affection between husbands and wives often ran deep. One European observer in New England told of a husband making a two-day, 40-mile trip just to fetch medicinal cranberries for his ill wife. Another noted that Abenaki widows often mourned their dead husbands for years and seldom remarried.

Young women became eligible for marriage as soon as they reached puberty. Young men could marry only after they had mastered the crafts of hunting and fishing and demonstrated that they could provide for a family. The passage from childhood to adulthood for both sexes was marked by ritual and ceremony. Upon menstruating for the first time, Lenape girls retired to a special hut, where they remained until they had menstruated again. Forbidden to touch their own hair or any food or eating utensils while in the hut, they draped a blanket over their head, ate with a stick, and drank from cupped hands. When they finally emerged from the hut, the girls donned a special headdress, signifying their eligibility for marriage.

Puberty rituals for boys were more demanding than those prescribed for girls. Powhatan boys between the ages of 10 and 15 who aspired to future leadership roles in their villages had to endure a rigorous and sometimes deadly initiation rite known as the Huskanaw. The proceedings began with dancing and feasting. Then as women mourned for them, the boys were led from the village by older males and symbolically sacrificed by men who danced around their seemingly lifeless bodies. For the next few months, the youngsters remained secluded in the forest under the watchful eye of keepers, who had already been initiated. During this time, the boys were beaten and made to drink a hallucinogenic herbal drink that so deranged them they had to be locked up in wooden cages.

Exhibiting the devotion to the young common among Algonquian families, a Penobscot mother rocks her baby in a hammock in the early 1900s. Specially crafted to hold infants securely, such hammocks were made of buckskin or blankets and padded with absorbent sphagnum moss.

Afterward, still dazed by the experience, they were returned to their families, who rejoiced in their "rebirth." Under their keepers' tutelage, they were then trained to be men. If an initiate showed any sign of remembering his earlier life or reverting to boyish ways, he was forced to undergo another Huskanaw, a challenge that often proved too much for him. Few boys survived two such ordeals in a row. Those who passed the test, however, were better prepared to serve as leaders among the Powhatan, who needed discipline to hold their chiefdom together and courage to defend their bountiful land against intruders.

Every tribe had its own courtship and marriage rituals. To propose marriage, a Maliseet man would toss a small stick or wood chip toward the woman he sought as his wife. The woman would pick up the chip, barely glancing at the man who tossed it, and look the gift over, as if wondering where it came from. If the offer was to her liking, she would toss the chip back to her suitor with a modest smile. If she disapproved of him, she would make a face and cast the chip disdainfully aside. A Lenape suitor proposed marriage by dispatching a respected emissary with presents of furs, food, and perhaps wampum to the young woman of his choice and her family. Acceptance of the gifts meant acceptance of the proposal; refusal meant the young man would have to look elsewhere for a wife.

The marriage ceremony itself often involved a dance and feast to which the entire village was invited. In Penobscot communities, the family of the groom hosted the event, which began in early evening and lasted until dawn. The newlyweds were then kept apart for two weeks, when another all-night dance and feast was held. These festivities ended with a ritual called Nada'buna, or Carrying the Bed, during which the groom brought his bedding to the bride's lodge, where the couple was finally left alone together. Some New England tribes encouraged trial marriages that allowed the couple to get to know each other under one roof while sleeping together chastely, head to foot. Not all groups had taboos against premarital sex, however, and nighttime liaisons between courting couples were common.

Although Algonquian marriages were usually monogamous, wealthy or prominent men sometimes had more than one wife. Among the Narragansett, most men of high standing practiced polygamy, in part because a husband was required to stay away from his wife from the time her pregnancy became known until the baby was weaned—a period that could be as long as three years. Narragansett women married to the same man usually lived in separate but adjacent houses. Among the Powhatan, leading men commonly had a number of wives and watched over them jealously.

Lower-ranking men were less possessive and sometimes allowed their wives to consort with other men, often out of courtesy to an honored guest. An illicit, or adulterous, relationship was one that took place without the husband's consent.

Like most Native Americans, Algonquians were indulgent parents and seldom punished their children. The Lenape believed that any mistreatment of children would anger the Creator and might cause the youngsters to be taken from their parents. Yet Algonquian children were remarkably well disciplined. From an early age, they learned through storytelling and the example of their elders that loud behavior, open displays of anger, and acts of selfishness brought shame and disapproval, while cooperation and generosity earned high praise. Children absorbed these lessons not only from their parents and siblings but also from an extended circle of grandparents, aunts and uncles, and cousins. Childhood events such as the first tooth, the first step, and, for boys, the killing of first game were marked by family celebrations. Should children become orphaned, they were immediately adopted by relatives. Children returned the affection and respect given them by their families by caring for their elders when they reached old age.

Most Algonquian tribes organized themselves by clan—a group of related families who traced their descent to a common ancestor, usually an animal. Clans derived their names from these animals, which also became the family's symbol. Turtle, bear, beaver, otter, and partridge clans, for example, were active among the Western Abenaki during the early 1700s. Abenakis believed that each family inherited certain characteristics from its ancestral animal; members of the Bear Clan, for instance, were believed to be especially wise, like the bear itself. Among tribes actively involved in trading with Europeans, clans claimed the rights to particular hunting grounds—privileges that were handed down from generation to generation. A Penobscot clan often marked its hunting range by painting or carving a likeness of its symbol on trees and rocks, or by posting birch-bark cutout silhouettes of its ancestral animal along the area's perimeters. Men sometimes tattooed their clan insignia on their cheeks as well.

In a 1585 drawing by John White, corn simmers in a clay stewpot. The pots were so well molded, wrote colonist Thomas Harriot, that English potters could "make no better."

In another drawing by White, a husband and wife wearing deerskin cloaks share a generous platter of hominy—an Algonquian term for hulled corn, which was boiled in kernel form or ground up and shaped into balls for cooking. "They make good cheer together," wrote Thomas Harriot of the southern Algonquians he and White encountered. "Yet are they moderate in their eating, whereby they avoid sickness. I would to God we would follow their example."

Much as certain clan rights and powers were inherited, tribal leadership often remained within a given family, passing from chiefs to their kin. Among the groups whose leaders inherited power were the Narragansett and Wampanoag of southern New England and the Piscataway, Nanticoke, and Powhatan around Chesapeake Bay. In some cases, the succession followed a prescribed order, proceeding through the chief's brothers and sisters and on to their children. In other cases, tribal councils selected the new leader from among several candidates belonging to the ruling family. Leaders who inherited their position often had broad powers. Among the Narragansett and tribes around the Chesapeake, for example, chiefs exacted tribute from their followers in the form of corn, deer hides, and other goods and could punish miscreants with their own hands. English colonists often referred to such imposing chiefs as kings or queens.

In northern New England, where people lived highly mobile and independent lives, leaders were beholden to their followers. Western Abenaki chiefs who acted weakly or dishonorably, for example, were stripped of power. But even in the far north, leadership was often inherited, and many chiefs played a commanding role in local affairs. Among the Micmac, noted an early French observer, the group leader was generally the "eldest son of some powerful family." This sagamore, as he was called, controlled the communal property and was expected to dispose of it wisely and generously. It was his responsibility "to provide dogs for the chase, canoes for transportation, provisions, and reserves for bad weather and expeditions." In return for such good services, hunters offered the sagamore part of their catch. Like his Abenaki counterparts, the Micmac sagamore sometimes met in council with neighboring chiefs and deliberated with them as equals, but in his own territory he knew no rival.

In southern New England, Algonquians called their chiefs sachems. Each tribe usually had one principal sachem, who presided over the entire group, and several lesser sachems, who governed the villages. Sachems administered justice, organized and hosted various rites and celebrations, received guests, allocated hunting and fishing lands, and served as diplomatic emissaries. Although they often inherited considerable power, they could ill afford to alienate their people. Tyrannical or incompetent chiefs soon lost their followers, who would leave and join another tribe. Here as among the Lenape, chiefs generally conferred with tribal members and with each other before reaching decisions. William Penn, who founded the Pennsylvania Colony and met often with Lenape chiefs, marveled at "how powerful the kings are, and yet how they move by the breath of their people."

Micmacs crafted these strings of tubular wampum beads from white and purple shells. Many coastal Algonquians fashioned similar wampum from quahogs, whelks, and other mollusk shells that littered their shores.

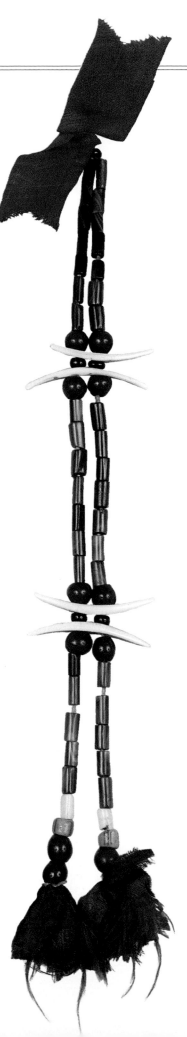

Farther south, where nature was especially generous with its gifts and some families grew wealthy and influential, tribal groups like the Powhatan were dominated by a ruling class with exceptional privileges. Most Powhatans were born into low-ranking families and remained commoners unless they performed great deeds and gained entry to the dominant class, made up of tribal chiefs called werowances, other members of the ruling family, priests, and accomplished hunters or warriors who served as advisers. Chiefs and their retinue lived in larger dwellings. On ceremonial occasions, they had servants to look after them, decked themselves out in pearls and precious furs, and entertained lavishly on the tribute they received. Upon death, chiefs were laid out in mortuary temples amid mounds of treasure and were said to have an exalted afterlife.

Even more powerful than the werowance was the *mamanatowick,* or paramount chief, who ruled over many tribes. Among the best known of these paramounts was Powhatan himself, who made a strong impression on early English colonists. Captain John Smith of the Jamestown Colony noted that lesser chiefs were obliged to yield part of the tribute they received to Powhatan, who amassed "skins, beads, copper, pearls, deer, turkeys, wild beasts, and corn." Smith likened Powhatan to an emperor, "who ruleth over many kings," and portrayed Powhatan's daughter Pocahontas as a princess—a notion that was later reinforced when Pocahontas married Jamestown colonist John Rolfe and sailed to England, where she charmed the royal family before dying of a disease she contracted there.

As paramount, Powhatan was by far the wealthiest man in his chiefdom. In each village, he had a large and well-stocked house, and often a wife or two. Colonists credited Powhatan with more than 100 wives during his lifetime, although he appears to have kept no more than a dozen with him at any one time. After a woman had his child, he would usually send her and the baby back to live with her family, although the child might later return to his household.

Whenever Powhatan traveled, Smith noted, he took along bodyguards—"40 or 50 of the tallest men his country doth afford"—who would stand vigil outside his dwelling. Any hapless guard who fell asleep while on duty was beaten. When Powhatan arrived at a village within his chiefdom, an elaborate welcoming celebration, complete with feasting, dancing, and speechmaking, was held. Men entertained him with vivid accounts of their hunting and war exploits. When he dined, noted an English observer, one woman brought him water in a wooden bowl to wash his hands, while another held a "bunch of feathers to wipe them instead of a towel."

Each spring, people planted a huge field for Powhatan amid great ceremony. By one account, the field covered 100 acres and yielded corn, beans, peas, gourds, and tobacco. After the planting, Powhatan circuited the field, walking backward and tossing wampum beads to his people, who scrambled for the treasure. From 1609 on, Powhatan conducted this annual rite wearing a paste-jewel crown sent to him by the king of England.

Although Powhatan and the chiefs under him had the authority to punish disobedient followers and execute wrongdoers, they always consulted their priests and advisers before declaring war or making other decisions affecting the tribe or the chiefdom as a whole. Rulers gave special weight to the advice of the priests, who were said to be able to foresee the future. Although priests sometimes married, they lived alone in temples, where they kept a fire perpetually burning. Using charms and medicinal herbs, they ministered to the sick. With their conjuring skills, they helped werowances determine the guilt or innocence of people accused of crimes. They organized ceremonies and managed the tribute paid to chiefs, which was often stored in the temple. Priests were allowed to hunt and fish, but

Dancing in a circle marked by carved posts, men and women holding branches and gourd rattles celebrate the summer green corn festival in another watercolor by John White depicting Algonquian life on the North Carolina coast.

A faithful reconstruction of a southern Algonquian village, situated near Jamestown, Virginia, features wigwams covered with reed mats (background) and a dance circle of seven posts (foreground, right), modeled after the one depicted by White. Each of the posts is carved with shroudlike drapery and a haunting face (inset), which may represent a spirit.

many lived on the offerings brought them by others, who were thankful for their services and fearful of their wrath. Priests kept in their temples images of a vengeful spirit called Okeus that were carried into battle.

Elsewhere, the decision to engage in battle was often made by war chiefs, who attained their positions not through inheritance but through brave deeds. War chiefs usually consulted with civil chiefs and others in the tribe before conducting warfare, which traditionally consisted largely of small-scale raids. Sometimes, a raid was undertaken to avenge a friend or relative killed or captured by the enemy. In other cases, the antagonism between rival tribes ran so deep that war chiefs required no special provocation to mount an expedition. Eager young men welcomed the chance to claim enemy scalps or captives and make a name for themselves.

Before Lenapes went off to war, they often hid their women and children on a small island or in a swamp to shield them from counterattacks. The men painted their faces and wore snakeskin headbands decorated with red turkey feathers or with wolf or foxtails. Attackers often crept up on enemy camps or villages at night and surprised their enemies while they slept. Occasionally rival war parties met in the open and traded shots with their bows from a distance or converged in a rush to hack at each other with clubs or tomahawks. But casualties were relatively few before Europeans introduced firearms. Victorious war parties returned virtually intact, bringing with them the scalps of a few unfortunate victims and a small number of prisoners. Men captured in battle were sometimes tortured and executed, but women and children were almost always adopted to replace lost relatives. Abenakis, like other groups, forced captives entering their villages to run a gantlet, but many prisoners got off lightly, receiving little more than taps on the shoulder. Adopted captives were cherished, for they were thought to embody the spirit of the loved ones they replaced.

The coastal tribes, like all Native American groups, believed that the world was alive with spirits, or manitous, as many Algonquians referred to them. The Narragansett ascribed to specific manitous control over men, women, children, animals, houses, the sun, moon, sea, fire, water, winds, directions, and even individual colors. Roger Williams counted 37 such "gods" among his Narragansett neighbors in the early 1600s, although they undoubtedly had more. The Narragansett also believed in a great creator—Cautantowwit—who, according to legend, sent a crow to their fields with the first seeds of corn and beans. For this reason, the Narragansett never harmed crows, no matter how much those birds pestered their gardens.

The stern face of a deity forms the head of this ceremonial Lenape war club. Such weapons were wielded by Algonquian fighting men during dances to signal their resolve and invoke spiritual aid.

Not all spirits were benevolent. Abenakis shared the widespread belief that underwater monsters lurked in their rivers and lakes, waiting to pull unwary fishermen out of their canoes and into a watery grave. They also believed that a huge birdlike creature named Pomola dwelt at the top of Mount Katahdin, the highest mountain in Maine, ready to swoop down and snatch away any person who displeased it. Among the Micmac's many deities was Skatekamuc, a ghostlike spirit whose appearance in a dream meant impending death. The Narragansett had a similar deity known as Cheepi, whose very name meant death. Associated with the cold northeast winds of winter and the color black, Cheepi appeared to humans most often at night in terrifying visions or dreams. He could transform himself into many forms, from inanimate objects to mythical creatures—and, in later times, even into the shape of Englishmen.

Anyone visited by a spirit heeded its message. Roger Williams wrote of a Wampanoag man who grew fearful when he felt the sun spirit send one of its beams into his chest. Taking it as a possible omen of death, he called together his friends and neighbors and maintained a sleepless vigil, fasting and praying for "10 days and nights." In the end, he was spared.

To appease the spirits that controlled all living things, Algonquians treated animals and plants with due respect. When raiding a muskrat's winter store of lily roots, for example, an Abenaki woman always left enough for the animal and offspring to survive on until spring. Before killing a deer or a bear—or even a tree—an Abenaki man prayed and apologized to the being's spirit. If Algonquians angered the spirit that watched over a given species, that creature might grow scarce. To avoid giving offense, people observed many taboos. A beaver's bones could not be carelessly thrown away, for example, but had to be buried or returned to the animal's native stream. Nor could the meat of any animal be wasted.

The first animal taken in the hunting season was often treated with special reverence. John McCullough, who was captured and adopted by Lenapes in the early 1800s, described the ritual hunters performed each year when they killed their first large buck. They would "cut the neck off the body, close to the shoulders," and carry the head home, "with the horns on." Then they kindled a large fire, placed the buck's head on the flames with its face toward the east, and circled the fire, singing and rattling a terrapin shell filled with small stones. Not until the head of the buck was consumed by fire would people feast on the animal's flesh.

Human spirits also had to be treated with respect after death. The Lenape believed that the souls of the dead went either west or south, where game was plenty and life easier. The Powhatan, on the other hand, thought the souls of their dead traveled east to the rising sun, the home of the Great Hare. A chief named Iopassus described that journey to Henry Spelman, a young Englishman who lived among the Powhatan in the early 1600s. Upon death, Iopassus said, the soul soars to the treetops, where it finds a broad, flat path stretching toward the eastern horizon, with berries and fruits growing on either side. The soul follows this inviting path toward the sun, stopping halfway at the wigwam of a gracious spirit who appears as a woman and offers corn, hickory-nut milk, and other refreshments. At the end of the journey, the soul reaches the land of the rising sun and the home of the Great Hare and finds ancestral spirits living there happily "in a goodly field, where they do nothing but dance and sing, and feed on delicious fruits with that Great Hare." After joining in these delights at length, the soul is ultimately reborn into the world of the living.

However they envisioned the afterlife, Algonquians took care to equip souls properly for their journey to the next world. The Lenape buried their dead with gifts of wampum beads, tools, food, and utensils. Although Lenapes conceived of the afterworld as a paradise, they mourned at length for their dead. Close relatives of the dead painted their faces black while in mourning. Widows sometimes grieved in that way for a full year, visiting the grave daily, where they threw themselves to the ground and wept. Women often singed their hair at the graves of their children. Long after the official mourning period had ended, relatives visited the burial places of their loved ones faithfully to keep the site clear of grass and weeds. Such attachment to the dead and their grave sites made the loss of ancestral territory to European colonists all the more painful.

Some tribes preferred to lay out the remains of the dead above ground, where the soul would be closer to heaven. Nanticokes and some neighboring groups placed the bodies of chiefs in a special lodge elevated on poles. Sometimes the body was mummified before being deposited there. After a period of mourning, the mummified body or bones were removed from the platform and buried. Some tribes gathered the bones of all their departed loved ones from separate burial pits every five to seven years and united them in a common grave or ossuary.

Algonquians expressed their communal faith and devotion in festive ways as well. At certain times of the year, they held ceremonies to thank the generous spirits and ask for their continued blessings. Each autumn, after the harvest, the Narragansett honored the creator Cautantowwit with a celebration that included sports, games, feasting, dancing, and gift

Wooden images such as this one, measuring about four feet high and representing a deity, were placed by southern Algonquians in temples near the remains of their chiefs. The Roanoke called their deity Kiwasa, while the Powhatan of Virginia knew theirs as Okeus. Depicted with a grim expression and draped with pearls, Okeus was closely identified with the spirit of dead rulers.

giving. For the occasion, Narragansetts constructed a ceremonial lodge up to 200 feet long near the chief sachem's house. A throng gathered there, and celebrants danced through the lodge and offered gifts to the poor. Other people burned prized possessions as offerings to Cautantowwit.

The Lenape had their own autumn rite, which was celebrated over a period of several days and included feasts of corn and venison. In the evenings, villagers gathered in a ceremonial lodge and danced in a circle to the pounding of hide drums. From time to time, people cast wampum or other valuables onto the dance floor for the benefit of the "poor and the fatherless," as one observer put it. In later times, when Lenapes had migrated far from their homeland, they honored tradition by performing an elaborate fall ritual known as the Big House Ceremony, performed in a longhouse that evoked the tribe's ancestral dwellings. Moving in a counterclockwise direction around a center post carved with masks representing the Creator, the worshipers danced, sang, and told of visions that brought them power from the spirit world.

Like other coastal groups, Lenapes believed that life arose from the sea. According to legend, the Creator coaxed a giant turtle from the bottom of the ocean. The turtle's back formed the earth, and the first people sprang from a great tree that took root there and reached all the way to heaven.

Lenape dancers impersonating the powerful spirit known as Mesingw, or the Keeper of Game, used regalia such as this early wooden mask, bearskin robe, turtle-shell rattle, and crooked staff.

A modern Lenape dancer impersonates Mesingw, wearing a traditional bearskin costume and a two-sided mask and carrying a turtle-shell rattle. Mesingw controlled the forest creatures and offered some of them to nourish devout Lenapes, who gave thanks by honoring the spirit in ceremonies. Once the dancer donned the costume, Lenapes said, he acquired the spirit's power, which endowed him with the ability to see in all directions and even cure diseases.

Creation legends varied from place to place, but many eastern Algonquians traced their origins to the Dawnland, where the sun rose from the sea. According to a Powhatan legend, the Great Hare created men and women and kept them in a bag at his home near the rising sun. He had good reason to be protective, for the spirits of the four winds visited his home, moaning with hunger and threatening to devour the humans. The Hare drove the winds away; then he formed land amid the waters and placed a single giant deer there for people to feast on. All too soon, however, the hungry winds swept down and consumed the deer, leaving nothing behind but the hide. Undeterred, the Hare took up the deer's pelt and carried it about, chanting a sacred song and scattering its hairs throughout the forest, where each strand became a small deer. The Great Hare knew now that his people would have plenty to eat and released them from his bag, sending men and women in pairs to different lands, where their descendants built snug shelters to keep out the winds and stalked the deer bequeathed to them.

In later times, when Europeans laid claim to much of the Algonquian homeland, tribespeople concluded sadly that the great creative spirits that watched over them had withdrawn in dismay to a distant place, where they would not be bothered by faithless intruders. Wonder-workers like Gluskab no longer walked the earth, although they still had their people in mind and promised one day to return.

Wampanoags on Martha's Vineyard told of their own benevolent giant, Maushop, who came to that island ages ago to avoid strife between tribes on the mainland. Maushop brought peace-loving Wampanoags with him to the island, and they lived quietly there until the giant dreamed that white people were coming to disturb them. Appalled by the prospect of renewed strife, Maushop decided to retreat to the sea. He gave his people a choice—they could either stay and face the intruders or follow him into the deep. Some chose to depart and were transformed by Maushop into whales. Others stayed behind and found themselves living as outcasts in their own country. Wampanoags who remained on the island said that they could still sense the presence of Maushop and his followers whenever fog swept in from the sea or whales appeared off the headlands. "They'll play around out there," one woman said of those kindred spirits, "then they'll disappear again. We think they're coming back to check on us to see how we are making out." ◆

TOMAH JOSEPH'S BIRCH BARK STORIES

Tomah Joseph, who crafted the alluring birch-bark designs on these pages, was born into the changing world of the Passamaquoddy in 1837. In the past, the Passamaquoddy of the Maine-New Brunswick border area had lived much like other Wabanakis of the region, cultivating some crops but relying mainly on fishing, hunting, and trapping, pursuits that required free access to a wide area. By Joseph's time, however, most of his people were relegated to small reservations in northeastern Maine and had to find new ways to subsist. Tomah Joseph did so with notable success. He became an expert hunting and fishing guide and adapted the age-old art of decorating birch bark to create objects for the tourist trade.

In the spring, Joseph loaded up his canoe with works he had crafted during the winter and paddled down the Saint Croix River into Passamaquoddy Bay, where he set up camp at Campobello Island, a fashionable resort area. There he sold his goods, performed traditional dances, and acted as a guide for prominent families such as the Roosevelts. Joseph was also an avid storyteller, and in the summer of 1882, he recounted many tribal legends for folklorist Charles Leland, who preserved them in print.

But it was by telling stories on birch bark that Tomah Joseph made his greatest contribution. He gathered the bark after the first hard freeze, when it was thicker, and incised designs on the dark inner layer to reveal the light outer layer, stitching the pieces together with spruce root to form useful objects. Traditionally, Passamaquoddies decorated birch bark with floral and geometric motifs, but Joseph portrayed scenes from the life and lore of his people to honor their traditions.

When Tomah Joseph died in 1914, at the age of 77, his birch-bark artistry was carried on by his son and grandson, who made their own contributions to an enduring culture.

A photograph of Tomah Joseph taken in the late 1800s appears in a birch-bark frame that he made himself and signed as governor of the Passamaquoddy, a position he held for several years. Joseph decorated many of his pieces with the image of an owl, portrayed at top left on the picture frame and on the birch-bark calling card above. The image served as a kind of trademark for Joseph and may have been a tribute to the creature he regarded as his spirit helper.

Joseph engraved this two-tiered picnic basket with scenes from legends and daily life. The top tier illustrates the story of a cunning ancestor named Fish, who foiled an attack on his kin by singing a magic song that caused each enemy warrior to grab the man in front by the hair and slay him with a tomahawk. The lower tier shows Passamaquoddies portaging canoes from one stream to another.

✦✦✦ CHARACTERS OF MYTH ✦✦✦

The fabled trickster and conjurer Rabbit, shown on the lid of the oval box below as a shaman smoking his pipe, figured prominently in the stories Tomah Joseph told in words and pictures. Atop the picture frame at right, Rabbit prepares to club Wicked Wildcat, his natural enemy, who set out to catch Rabbit for dinner only to fall victim himself. The middle scene depicts Passamaquoddies canoeing past Friar's Rock on Campobello. The bottom image may represent the giant called Gluskab in the act of banishing White Bear for threatening humans.

This box lid portrays Gluskab with a magic pipe he used to lure animals, crossing the sea in his canoe with his grandmother, who was known to Passamaquoddies as Munimkwes, or Woodchuck. The inscription reads, "Woodchuck Sits in a Stone Canoe."

At the center of this richly decorated wall pocket sits the figure of a "mikamwes," one of the "wondrous dwellers in the lonely woods" that Joseph celebrated in his stories. Among other attributes, these little people were said to be the source of magic pipes. To the right, Joseph inscribed two Passamaquoddy sayings: "kolele mooke," which means "good luck," and "mikwid hamin," or "remember me."

✦✦✦ SCENES FROM THE HUNT ✦✦✦

Tomah Joseph, shown here drawing his bow, expressed his love of hunting on this frame and on many other objects he crafted. Feather headdresses like the ones he posed in and portrayed in his work were worn by Passamaquoddies primarily for ceremony or display.

Two hunting scenes—a man stalking a moose on snowshoes and another carrying a deer home in a canoe—adorn this magazine holder, signed and dated by the artist. Wabanakis on snowshoes could overtake a moose lumbering through deep snow.

Joseph decorated even the back of this picture frame in great detail, portraying men on snowshoes stalking a deer (top), then one of the hunters dragging the animal home on a rope. The same hunter arrives with his catch (bottom), to be greeted by his expectant family.

A fisherman returns to his lodge where a woman tends a cooking pot in this scene incised by Joseph atop a glove box. He surrounded the camp scene with traditional floral and geometric patterns and graced the sides of the box with images of woodsmen and wildlife.

✦✦✦ THE WATERY WORLD ✦✦✦

Tomah Joseph posed for this photograph in his canoe—an essential tool of his trade as a guide as well as a recurring motif in his birch-bark designs.

A man makes a portage with a canoe on his shoulders on this collar box, used to hold the detachable shirt collars men wore in Joséph's day.

Joseph decorated this canoe backrest with a camp scene featuring his familiar owl (top), labeled here in Passamaquoddy as "koko-gus." Below, a woman with a parasol leans against a backrest much like this one, while her canoe, paddled by two men, slips past Friar's Rock on Campobello.

This 50-inch-long birch-bark model canoe is inscribed with a variety of animals that frequented the woods and waterways the artist knew so well—including a wildcat, a beaver outside its lodge, a fox, fish, and turtles.

✦✦✦ A CONTINUING TRADITION ✦✦✦

Tomah Joseph's son Sabattis, pictured above with a decorated canoe paddle, carried on the birch-bark artistry of his father. The wastebasket shown at right is one of many pieces by Sabattis, who echoed themes used by Tomah Joseph but evolved a style of his own.

This oval box adorned with an image of the little wonder-worker Mikamwes and Wicked Wildcat was made in 1990 by Joe Murphy, Tomah Joseph's grandson. Murphy applied new technology to the task, using a wood-burning tool instead of the conventional cutting tool.

In 1993 descendants of Tomah Joseph gathered at the Robert Abbe Museum in Bar Harbor, Maine, to celebrate the opening of an exhibition of Joseph's work entitled "History on Birch Bark." In addition to Joseph's son and grandson, other family members have perpetuated the traditional Passamaquoddy crafts.

M. Swett invt. et Del.

Lith. of Pendleton.

BLACK WILLIAM selling NAHANT

to Thomas Dexter for a Suit of Clothes.

1630.

2

CONFRONTING THE COLONISTS

An Algonquian known to English colonists as Black William accepts clothing as payment for the peninsula of Nahant in Massachusetts Bay. Colonial authorities denied the legality of such purchases on the grounds that the land belonged to the Crown and no title could be obtained from Indians "on pretense of their being native proprietors."

On March 22, 1621, Massasoit, the chief sachem of the Wampanoag, appeared with 60 of his warriors at the fledgling English colony of New Plymouth on Massachusetts Bay. Massasoit had come in peace, but the colonists were wary. Since landing in Plymouth harbor the previous December in search of religious sanctuary, the Puritans had been reduced by disease and hunger from 101 men, women, and children to scarcely half that number. Moreover, they had heard tales of Indian hostility from earlier visitors to the region that were enough to make them "quake and tremble," in the words of William Bradford, the colony's future governor. Daunted by Massasoit's sizable contingent, the Puritans were inclined to keep the Wampanoags at a distance—until an unlikely intermediary stepped forward with welcoming words. Known as Tisquantum, or Squanto, he was a Wampanoag by birth, but he had mastered the English language. Indeed, he had learned more about Europeans in a few eventful years than most colonists would learn about Algonquians in a lifetime.

Tisquantum had grown up in the Wampanoag village of Pawtuxet on Plymouth harbor when European ships were already visiting the coast of New England to fish, trade, or plunder. In 1614 an English captain named Thomas Hunt raided the area and abducted Tisquantum and 23 other Indians. Hunt sold them into slavery at the Spanish port of Málaga, but Tisquantum escaped and reach England, where he was taken in by John Slany, treasurer of the company overseeing England's first colony in North America, on Newfoundland. Under Slany's patronage, Tisquantum ventured to Newfoundland and back. Then, in 1619, he sailed with an English expedition to Cape Cod as pilot. Soon after the party made landfall, he went off to rejoin his kin at Pawtuxet, only to discover that the village had been wiped out by an epidemic of European origin that swept the coast a few years earlier. The Puritans at Plymouth harbor found human bones strewn about deserted Wampanoag dwellings, where no one had been left to bury the dead.

Soon after that dismal homecoming, Tisquantum arrived at New Plymouth with Massasoit and served as interpreter for talks between the

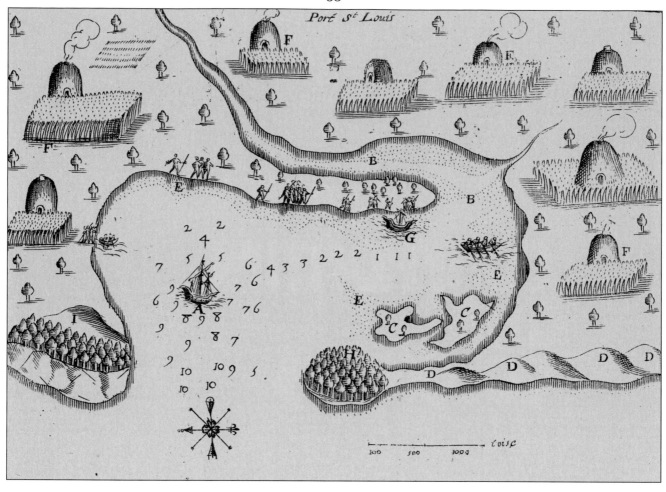

Port St Louis

chief and the Puritans. The recent epidemic had unsettled the Wampanoag and left them vulnerable to rival groups, notably the Narragansett to their west, who had come through the crisis relatively unscathed. Massasoit was eager for an alliance with the English, and Tisquantum helped arrange that pact. Afterward, he chose to remain at New Plymouth, on his native ground. In the words of William Bradford, he "continued with them, and was their interpreter, and was a special instrument sent of God for their good beyond their expectation. He directed them how to set their corn, where to take fish, and to procure other commodities, and was also their pilot to bring them to unknown places for their profit, and never left them till he died."

But Tisquantum's stay among the Puritans from the spring of 1621 until his death of disease in late 1622 was not altogether peaceful or secure. He was caught between two worlds, and he tried with mixed success to wield influence among Wampanoags as well as colonists. In one instance, a relative of his told the Puritans that Massasoit had joined with the Narragansett in a plot to destroy the colony. Massasoit angrily denied the charge, and both he and the Puritans concluded that Tisquantum had fabricated the claim to undermine Massasoit and strengthen his own position as a tribal spokesman. On another occasion, Tisquantum assured Wampanoags

A chart drawn in July 1605 by French explorer Samuel de Champlain portrays Port Saint Louis—or Plymouth harbor, as the English called it—where Wampanoag villagers passed the summer in wigwams dispersed amid the cornfields. A European-borne epidemic swept the coast a dozen years or so after Champlain's visit, leaving the area depopulated when the Pilgrims landed here in 1620.

that he had power over the colonists because he knew the origin of the dread disease they spread among Indians. The source of the plague was buried beneath the storehouse in New Plymouth, he insisted, and he would have much to say about how the colonists made use of it in the future.

Tisquantum's disturbing tale—perhaps intended to enhance his stature among Wampanoags—was not entirely without foundation. The colonists had buried kegs of gunpowder beneath the storehouse to safeguard that deadly material. When anxious Wampanoags related Tisquantum's story to the colonists, they denied that the kegs contained disease but insisted that their God indeed had the power to inflict the plague "upon those that should do any wrong to his people." Tisquantum had seen the terrible effect of that scourge on his people at Pawtuxet, and he had come to terms with the intruders and their God. Yet he was not merely an "instrument" of the colony, as Bradford put it. Like other resourceful Algonquians who reached an accommodation with alien powers in these difficult times, he claimed some authority over the newcomers and made them beholden to him.

From the time strangers first appeared off their shores in great ships, Algonquians tried to deal peacefully with them. The Europeans came from across the sea, from the Dawnland, and most coastal tribes were eager to share in the strangers' remarkable gifts and offer them presents in return. Only when the visitors acted in a way unbefitting honored guests did their hosts begin to distrust them. That Algonquians were otherwise well disposed to Europeans was confirmed by Giovanni da Verrazano, an Italian navigator who sailed up the East Coast in the spring of 1524 searching for a sea passage to China. He explored the fine harbor below the island of Manhattan, where Lenapes on shore expressed joy and wonderment and gestured for him to land. Strong winds prevented him from doing so, but he later entered Narragansett Bay and spent 15 days among curious and hospitable Narragansetts. "These people are the most beautiful and have the most civil customs we have found on this voyage," he wrote. "Their manner is sweet and gentle, very like the manner of the ancients."

As Verrazano continued up the coast, however, he encountered Indians who had

This reconstructed Wampanoag wigwam, covered with reed mats and insulated with rushes for occupation in winter, was erected at Plimoth Plantation in Massachusetts. It represents the homesite of Hobomock, who lived among the Plymouth colonists with his family as one of their interpreters and guides.

reason to fear white men. Europeans had been haunting the shores of the Abenaki, Micmac, and other northern Algonquians—known collectively as Wabanakis—for some time, mainly to harvest codfish but also to barter with coastal tribes or make off with what they wanted. Some of those intruders had abducted Indians and left behind trails of disease. Thus when Verrazano encountered Eastern Abenakis along the Maine coast, they were neither curious nor congenial. When the sailors tried to go ashore, they were met with a barrage of arrows. One coastal village finally agreed to exchange goods with the Europeans, but only from a distance. Standing atop a rocky cliff, the Abenakis used a long rope to lower a basket of trade goods to several members of Verrazano's crew, who bobbed about in a small boat. "We found no courtesy in them," wrote Verrazano, and he sailed away convinced that these Indians were "bad people."

Those Abenakis had reason to be wary of all visiting ships. But elsewhere, Algonquians generally distinguished between hostile and friendly factions and gave newcomers the benefit of the doubt. Tribes demonstrated that they were willing not only to trade with Europeans but also to tolerate them as neighbors. Many early colonies would have collapsed without Indian aid, and few met with concerted resistance until they violated the trust of Algonquians by challenging their beliefs, defying their leaders, or claiming their land.

The first attempts by Europeans to settle among Algonquians occurred to the south. In 1570 Spanish Jesuits founded a mission on Virginia's York River. At the time, Chief Powhatan was a young man and had yet to establish control over many tribes. The Jesuits dealt instead with a high-ranking Algonquian they called Don Luis, who had been picked up along the coast by a

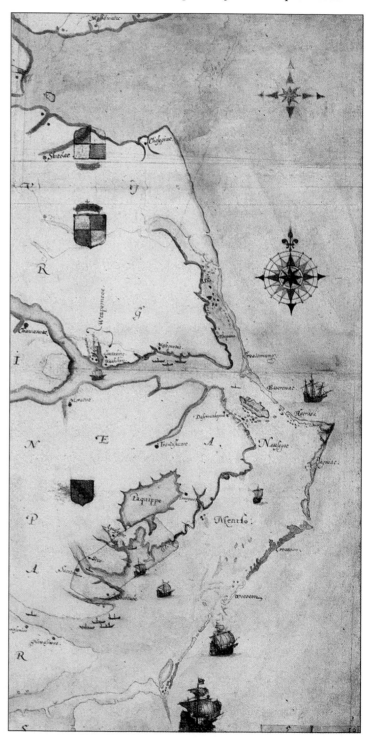

A map painted in 1585 by John White—who accompanied the first English expedition to the North Carolina coast that year and returned as leader of the second expedition in 1587—shows the location of various Algonquian villages and foraging grounds from Chesapeake Bay south to Cape Lookout.

Spanish ship 10 years earlier and converted to Catholicism. Jesuits then accompanied him back to his homeland to start a mission with his help. Like Tisquantum, however, Don Luis still longed, after living among Europeans, to be respected by his own people. A few days after the Spanish party arrived, he slipped away and resumed his former life as a noble Algonquian, taking several wives, which shocked the Jesuits when they learned about it.

Without Don Luis, the mission languished. The Jesuits bartered with neighboring Indians, but they failed to attract the converts they needed to sustain their community. In desperation, three priests made the fatal error of seeking out Don Luis and trying to pressure him into returning. Such a concession would have subjected Don Luis to scorn, and the mere presence of alien priests at his side may have been humiliating for him. He reacted by rallying warriors who attacked and killed the three priests, then put to death five other Jesuits at the mission site. The following year, a punitive expedition arrived from the West Indies and claimed the lives

In a watercolor by White, Secotans—neighbors of the Roanoke on the North Carolina coast—gather around a fire with gourd rattles in hand to thank the spirits for their bounty. The Roanoke, who were commonly blessed with good harvests, wondered why the God that the colonists prayed to left them dependent on others for subsistence.

of many Indians in return, bringing to a bloody end Spanish efforts to colonize the area.

Algonquians in Virginia would not soon forget the punitive expedition, but tribes to their south later proved receptive to foreigners of another nationality. In 1585 Roanokes along the coast of North Carolina welcomed a party of English settlers to Roanoke Island, situated between the

This 23-year-old Virginia Algonquian was portrayed about 1640 while visiting London as a guest of the English. He wears a headband of animal claws and a necklace similar to the one above, crafted in Virginia from half-inch-long marginella shells. Shell beads served as currency in exchanges between Indians and early Virginia colonists.

mainland and the Outer Banks. In exchange for metal tools and other valued gifts, Roanokes allowed the visitors to build shelters on the island, furnished them with food, and showed them how to construct weirs to catch fish. By the following spring, however, the needy colonists had made themselves a burden to their hosts by demanding food at a time when the Roanoke had little to spare and were suffering from diseases communicated by the colonists. Amid growing resentment, the settlers received word that Indians were plotting against them and responded by attacking and killing the Roanoke chief, Wingina, and a number of his followers. Wary of reprisals, the settlers retreated to England in June 1586. A second group of 100 or so colonists landed on Roanoke Island a year later, but they faced considerable hostility and hardship. By the time a relief ship reached the colony from England three years later, the site was deserted. The fate of the lost colonists remained a mystery.

In 1607 another party of colonists sailed up the mouth of the James River in Virginia and founded the first permanent English settlement in North America, Jamestown. The colonists named that site and the river it bordered after their king, James I. But the real authority they had to reckon with was Chief Powhatan, who was then about 60 years of age and at the peak of his power. Powhatan had mixed feelings about the intruders. He was well aware of earlier troubles stirred up by white men along the coast. As a paramount chief of great resourcefulness, however, he was confident that he could soon bring the strangers under control much as he had subject tribes, either by forcing them to submit or by persuading them to join his chiefdom voluntarily and pay him tribute.

Barely two weeks after the Jamestown colonists arrived, Powhatan tested the newcomers by sending a group of warriors to attack their partially constructed settlement. The Englishmen repelled the warriors with muskets and forced them back into the woods. Other, deadlier skirmishes followed, interspersed with peaceful exchanges. As Powhatan learned more about the determined colonists and the goods at their disposal, he saw the advantages of luring them into his chiefdom. He pursued that possibility in December 1607, when Captain John Smith of the Jamestown Colony was captured by his warriors and brought before him. Smith later claimed that it was only through the intercession of Powhatan's young daughter, Pocahontas, that he escaped being executed by Powhatan's armed men on the spot. In all likelihood, however, the chief simply wanted to overawe his captive before offering him a deal. Prior to releasing him, Powhatan assured Smith that they were now friends and promised that if the English paid him tribute in the form of a grindstone and "two great guns," he would grant Smith control of the Powhatan village of Capahosic and the surrounding territory and "forever esteem him as his son."

Considering that Smith was in no position to bargain, it was a generous offer. But accepting would have defined him as Powhatan's subordinate, and like other ambitious colonists, Smith was intent on mastering the land and its native inhabitants. A few months later, he made a diplomatic visit to Powhatan and asked for the promised territory even though he failed to produce the two great guns, or cannon, the paramount chief expected. Powhatan countered Smith's request by insisting that the English first lay down their arms, "as did his subjects." The colonists would never defer to the chief in this manner, and diplomacy soon gave way to renewed conflict.

In 1613 another chance for peace arose when a party of Englishmen lured Pocahontas aboard their ship while she was visiting an independent tribe to the north, the Patawomeck, whose leaders aided in her abduction under pressure from the English. The capture of Pocahontas and her subsequent marriage to colonist John Rolfe helped persuade Powhatan to come to terms with the English. Hoping to reinforce the accord, the Virginia colony's governor, Thomas Dale, proposed marrying a younger daughter of Powhatan, but the chief rejected him. He would never willingly enter an English settlement, and he did not care to lose touch with another daughter. "I am old now and would gladly end my days in peace," he assured the colonists, adding that if they threatened him, "my country is large enough, I will remove myself farther from you."

By the time Powhatan died in 1618, however, his domain was dwindling and his people were being drawn closer to the English and their ways. Many of them prized English trade goods, in particular tools and firearms, and some Powhatans became part of the English economy, toiling for colonists in their homes or fields. The successful cultivation in Virginia of an imported variety of tobacco—a cash crop introduced by John Rolfe that helped enrich his descendants by Pocahontas but did little to help others of Indian ancestry—greatly increased English encroachment on tribal territory. Even the spiritual foundation of the Powhatan began to erode as colonists inaugurated efforts to convert them to Christianity. And a recent epidemic had devastated some villages and made it harder for Powhatans to subsist in the traditional manner.

These changes alarmed many Algonquians who recalled how things had been before the English arrived and longed to restore the chiefdom to its former might. In 1622 Powhatan's brother Opechancanough, who

One of the wyues of Wyngyno.

IMAGES OF A HEROINE

The story of Pocahontas, the Powhatan Indian girl who became the heroine of the Jamestown Colony, remains one of America's most enduring legends—one attended by few hard facts. The account of her rescuing Captain John Smith from execution at the hands of her father's warriors is probably fanciful. But for certain her marriage to the planter John Rolfe restored relations between her people and the colonists; many of Virginia's first families trace their ancestry back to that union. Just as the facts of her life are elusive, so is her countenance. Artists through the years have rendered the Pocahontas of their dreams, a face befitting an undying legend of feminine virtue.

MATOAKA ALS REBECCA FILIA POTENTISS : PRINC : POWHATANI IMP: VIRGINIÆ .

Ætatis suæ 21. A. 1616

Matoaks als Rebecka daughter to the mighty Prince Powhatan Emperour of Attanoughskomouck als virginia converted and baptized in the Christian faith, and wife to the worth Mr. Joh: Rolff.

Si: Pass: sculp: Compton Holland excud:

The real Poca-
hontas probably
wore a buckskin
apron, body paint,
and tattoos similar
to those of this
Algonquian woman
rendered by John
White, who in 1585
became a member
of the first English

The Powhatan Guards, a militia unit formed in 1860 in Powhatan County, Virginia, to fight in the Civil War, carried this ceremonial banner bearing a portrait of Pocahontas. The unit subsequently became Company E of the 4th Virginia Cavalry. The Virginia state seal is on the reverse side of the flag.

Pocahontas became a popular name given to racehorses. A number of 19th-century female thoroughbreds were named after her, including this world champion pacing mare shown pulling a sulky in an 1857 engraving.

An image of Pocahontas appears opposite a portrait of George Washington on a $100 Commonwealth of Virginia Treasury note issued during the Civil War. Many Southerners saw the pair as the symbolic father and mother of the Confederacy, thus establishing an American identity for themselves that was separate from that of their Northern adversaries.

A comely, regal Pocahontas disdains an English suitor in this 1911 oil painting by Howard Chandler Christy. The artist developed a style of portraying women as sensuous yet independent and strong willed—a profile that suited the Pocahontas of legend.

Carved from pine, this Pocahontas figurehead adorned an early-19th-century merchant ship or whaler. The headdress and tobacco leaves were probably added when the sculpture was removed from the ship and converted into a cigar-store Indian.

was now paramount chief, led a well-coordinated campaign against the English that testified to his enduring hold over the area's tribes. Hundreds of colonists died in the initial assaults, but the English recovered and struck back with a vengeance, dealing the Powhatans a major defeat in 1624. In years to come, more colonists poured into Virginia to cultivate tobacco, and the English strengthened their grip on Powhatan territory.

After putting down one last uprising by the elderly Opechancanough in the 1640s, colonists imposed terms that defined Powhatan leaders as vassals of the English king and required them to pay annual tribute to the colony's governor. Within a few decades, only 11 of the 28 tribes that John Smith had tallied in 1608 still existed in the Virginia colony. Of the 15,000 or more Powhatans who had inhabited the area when the English first came ashore at Jamestown, merely 2,000 or so remained, crowded onto small parcels of land assigned to them by the colony—the first Indian reservations in North America. Nor were those reservations secure from intrusions. Colonists let their livestock loose to graze on Indian crops and attacked Powhatans who protested; squatted on tribal land; purchased lots and then refused to pay for them; or used corrupt interpreters to manipulate Indians into selling land when they thought they were signing documents that simply confirmed their right of possession.

While the struggle for Tidewater Virginia was playing out, another English colony was starting up in Maryland. Among the first settlers there were Catholics seeking refuge from persecution in England. In 1634 they built the fortified village of Saint Marys on the river of that same name that flowed south into the Potomac near its mouth. The dominant tribe in the area was the Piscataway, whose chief presided as paramount over several other groups along the north bank of the Potomac. The Piscataway chiefdom was smaller and more vulnerable than the one controlled by Powhatan when Jamestown was settled. Wedged between the growing Virginia colony to the south and assertive Susquehannocks to the north—Iroquoian speakers who frequented the area to raid and trade—the Piscataway were eager for an alliance with the oncoming Marylanders. To signal his good intentions, the paramount converted to Catholicism in the late 1630s, urged his followers to do likewise, and even granted Maryland authorities the right to appoint his successors.

Unfortunately, alliance with the Maryland colonists only put the Piscataway at greater peril. Dutch and Swedish colonists in what is now Delaware were eager to cause trouble for the upstart Marylanders and supplied firearms to the Susquehannock, who mounted deadly attacks on

Pictured in the late 1890s, members of the Pamunkey tribe—once part of Powhatan's chiefdom—wear stylized Indian dress for performances they staged to dramatize the legend of John Smith and his rescue by Pocahontas. After shattering the Powhatan chiefdom in the mid-1600s, Virginia authorities allotted the Pamunkey a small reservation and made them pay tribute each year to show that they were subject to the English.

the Piscataway and their Maryland allies. The colony survived with the help of fresh infusions of English settlers, but the Piscataway never regained their former strength. Many who endured the raids fell prey to European-borne diseases or were displaced by the very colonists they had looked to for support. Once the western side of Chesapeake Bay was well settled, newcomers from England overspread Maryland's Eastern Shore, where the Nanticoke soon lost much of their territory.

To the north, Lenapes living along the Delaware River in present-day New Jersey and Pennsylvania also felt pressure from Susquehannocks, who sought to dominate trade with Europeans probing upriver from Delaware Bay. But the first Lenapes to come in close and prolonged contact with white colonists were those living along the lower Hudson River. That waterway had been explored in 1609 by the English navigator Henry Hudson, who was seeking a passage to China for a Dutch trading company. As he ventured upriver, Hudson first encountered Lenapes and later Mahicans, who greeted him with "good cheer," as he put it, and carried him to their chief's house, where they honored him with strings of

The coat of arms of New Amsterdam pays tribute to the beaver—whose valuable pelt inspired Dutch fur traders to found this colony at the mouth of the Hudson River in 1625. Lenapes in the area welcomed traders but resented the arrival of Dutch farmers who infringed on tribal territory.

wampum. They also offered him beaver and otter skins in return for glass beads, knives, hatchets, and liquor.

When news of the sleek hides Hudson received reached Amsterdam, other Dutch ships set sail, eager to launch a fur-trading business in the New World. By the 1620s, the Dutch had established several important fur-trading posts in the mid-Atlantic region, including one at the mouth of the Hudson River called New Amsterdam. Peter Minuit supposedly purchased that site by offering the local Lenapes beads and other items worth 60 guilders to the Dutch, or about 24 dollars by 20th-century American standards. At the time, however, the sale of land had no meaning in Algonquian culture. The Lenapes probably regarded the payment as a consideration that was due them for tolerating the presence of the visitors and allowing them to make use of the land for a while. Indeed, Dutch officials in their instructions to Minuit envisioned the payment not as a transaction but as a way of courting native hospitality. They told him not to drive away the island's inhabitants "by force or threats," but to persuade them by kind words "or otherwise by giving them something, to let us live amongst them."

For a while, the relationship between the Dutch at New Amsterdam and their Algonquian hosts remained cordial. By the late 1630s, however, Dutch farmers as well as traders were streaming into New Amsterdam and environs, and the colonists began to make themselves unwelcome. Tensions mounted and finally erupted in 1642 when a band of Hackensack Lenapes living across the Hudson from New Amsterdam killed two Dutch farmers who had traded sharply with them and allowed cattle to roam free and trample their corn. The Hackensack chiefs offered to give the widow of one of the murdered men wampum to "wipe away her tears," as was their custom in such cases, but Dutch officials rejected the proposal. They demanded that the murderers be handed over to them, and the Lenapes refused. After a yearlong standoff, Dutch officials dispatched 80 soldiers to arrest the farmers' killers. Instead of bringing back the Hackensack men responsible for the murders, however, the soldiers attacked another band of Lenapes, who had taken refuge in the area after being driven downriver by rival Mahicans equipped with firearms. The soldiers massacred those refugees, killing every man, woman, and child.

Two decades of sporadic violence ensued as Lenapes clashed with both Dutch soldiers and Mahicans, who profited by the fur trade and became the dominant tribe in the region before yielding to the Iroquois in the 1670s. By that time, the English had wrested New Amsterdam from the Dutch and renamed it New York, and the once populous Lenape bands in the area had dwindled or dispersed. Those Indians who remained struggled to eke out a living, often laboring on Dutch or English farms to support themselves. Colonist Daniel Denton wrote in 1670 that the few Indians left on Manhattan Island were in "no ways hurtful but

In the earliest known view of New Amsterdam, Lenapes in a canoe approach Dutchmen in a launch. As indicated by the fort at the foot of Manhattan Island, the colonists were prepared for opposition from resentful Algonquians and rival Europeans.

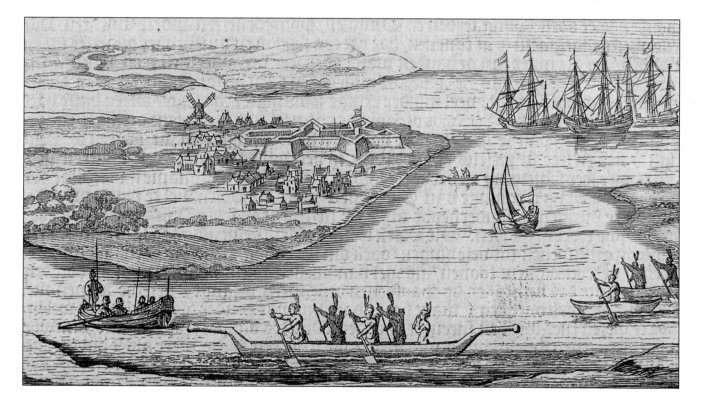

rather serviceable to the English." Like other colonists, he saw the woes of the surrounding Algonquians as the work of Providence: "It is to be admired, how strangely they have decreased by the hand of God."

With the departure of the Dutch, the English became the dominant European faction for Algonquians to reckon with everywhere but in the north, where the French had forged strong trading ties with the Wabanaki. Although French mariners were among the Europeans who aroused early resentment in tribes along the coast of Maine and New Brunswick, French traders and missionaries soon learned by necessity to be more diplomatic. They planted small and scattered settlements in eastern Canada and what is now northern New England. By 1640, after several decades of colonizing attempts, the French population throughout North America numbered only 270, hardly enough to challenge Algonquians for their land. French traders needed the cooperation of Wabanaki hunters to provide a continuous supply of beaver pelts—the mainstay of the fur trade. To strengthen their ties to tribal groups, the traders often took Indian wives, who were expert at processing hides and performing other useful tasks and kept their husbands company at the lonely outposts.

A far different challenge faced Wampanoags, Narragansetts, and neighboring Algonquians in southern New England. There English colonists saw their new home as a wilderness and set out to redeem it—a task that involved assimilating or sweeping aside tribal groups who had not already been devastated by epidemics like the one that left Plymouth harbor open for settlement by the Puritans in 1620. As William Bradford wrote of that calamity, "There is neither man, woman, nor child remaining, as indeed we have found none, so that there is none to hinder our possession." Elsewhere in the area, Algonquians were still numerous, but despite ample evidence to the contrary, colonists asserted that the Indians simply roamed from place to place and had no claim to the land. To keep peace, officials of the Massachusetts Bay Colony—founded in 1630 within the territory of the Massachusett, who lived north of the Wampanoag—made it a practice to purchase land from Indians who might "pretend any title" to a particular site. But most English colonists were convinced that this new country belonged to their God and king and that Indians belonged there only if they accepted Christianity and became useful subjects.

In the early years of colonization, the settlers in southern New England were too few to impose their will on surrounding Algonquians and had to enter into alliances with them that entangled both sides in unforeseen complications. The agreement that Plymouth colonists reached with Chief Massasoit of the Wampanoag, for example, nearly involved them in war with the formidable Narragansett, who claimed authority over the Wampanoag. Such a conflict might have been ruinous for the struggling Puritans, but they were spared the test, largely because the Narragansett were diverted by challenges from another group, the Pequot of Connecticut. By the 1630s, the Pequot were trading energetically with the Dutch and asserting control over neighboring tribes such as the Niantic near Long Island Sound, from whom they claimed tribute in wampum. To Canonicus, the chief sachem of the Narragansett, the expansive Pequot were even more worrisome than the English. Ultimately the Narragansett were drawn into an alliance with the colonists against the Pequot, whom the English saw as an obstacle to their plans for a new colony in Connecticut.

The Englishman who sealed that fateful alliance was Roger Williams, a clergyman who learned the language of the Narragansett, viewed their culture sympathetically, and believed that no Christian had the God-given right to occupy land unless he first came to terms with the native inhabitants. Banished from the Massachusetts Bay Colony in 1635 for doctrinal disputes with authorities, he left with a number of followers and founded the colony of Rhode Island the following spring, settling at the site he called Providence on land purchased from Canonicus. As governor, Williams tried to be fair to the Narragansett, but he was also committed to English colonization and promoted that cause in his dealings with the tribe.

In September 1636, fighting broke out between the Pequot and the English in Connecticut. Fearing for his own colony and for the safety of neighboring settlers, Williams hastened to enlist the support of the Narragansett. He conferred with Chief Miantonomi—the nephew of Canonicus and his diplomatic spokesman—who was even then being urged by emissaries from the Pequot to unite with them against the colonists. "Three days and nights my business forced me to lodge and mix with the bloody Pequot ambassadors," Williams wrote afterward. In the end, he prevailed, and the Narragansett sided with the English in a campaign that augured ill for all native New Englanders. In May 1637, about 90 armed English colonists and hundreds of warriors, many of them Narragansetts, surrounded a Pequot village on the Mystic River and set fire to it, slaughtering those who tried to escape. Several hundred men, women, and children died in the massacre. Those few Pequots who survived were sold into slavery in the West Indies. To Narragansetts, who regarded any battle toll of more

THE FIRST THANKSGIVING

Very little is known about the first Thanksgiving at Plymouth. Pilgrim Father Edward Winslow only briefly described the occasion in a letter written to friends in England in 1621. "Our harvest being gotten in, our governor sent four men on fowling, that we might, after a special manner, rejoice together after we had gathered the fruit of our labors," he wrote. "At which time, amongst other recreations, we exercised our arms, many Indians coming amongst us, and among the rest their greatest king, Massasoit, with some 90 men, whom for three days we entertained and feasted; and they went out and killed five deer, which they brought to the plantation, and bestowed on our governor, and on the captain and others."

The happy event celebrated a harvest that signaled the end of a very lean period for the Pilgrims. Nearly half of the original 102 colonists had died of disease and exposure since their arrival less

than a year before. With the help of the Wampanoag Indians, they were able to learn the best ways to hunt, fish, and effectively raise 20 acres of Indian corn, in fields that the Indians had cleared long before their arrival. For nearly 50 years more, the two cultures would find a way to coexist, until King Philip's War poisoned Indian-white relations and decimated the Wampanoag tribe.

In that first year, however, the colonists owed their survival to help from the Indians. This fact influenced Native American artist Murv Jacob in rendering his own version of Thanksgiving. In Jacob's painting, the event takes place at a palisaded Wampanoag village under a colorful canopy of bright autumn leaves. The Indians are the hosts, Pilgrims the guests. Cooking fires are blazing; trays and baskets of provender have been laid out. Children romp, and Indians and colonists sit together as equals to share the bounty.

The Reverend John Eliot of the Massachusetts Bay Colony (left) began his mission work there in the 1640s by learning the native language of the Massachusett tribe with the assistance of a gifted Indian named Cochenoe, who was fluent both in English and in various Algonquian dialects. Eliot later translated the Bible into a written version of the Massachusett tongue. When the translation appeared in 1663 (below), it was the first Bible of any kind printed in North America.

MAMUSSE
WUNNEETUPANATAMWE
UP-BIBLUM GOD
NANEESWE
NUKKONE TESTAMENT
KAH WONK
WUSKU TESTAMENT.

Ne quoſhkinnumuk naſhpe Wuttinneumoh *CHRIST*
noh aſoowefit

JOHN ELIOT·

CAMBRIDGE:
Printeuoop naſhpe *Samuel Green* kah *Marmaduke Johnſon.*
1 6 6 3.

than a few lives as steep, the carnage was sobering. They asked to adopt some of the captured Pequots into their own tribe, as was their custom following a battle, but the English refused and the prisoners were enslaved.

The war was a triumph for the English, clearing the way for colonization of Connecticut, but it left the Narragansett in a precarious position. For years to come, they feuded with the Mohegan—a tribal group in Connecticut who had broken away from the Pequot and supported the colonists. And they feared the English, realizing that what had happened to their old foes could also happen to them. By 1640 Miantonomi had become chief sachem of the Narragansett and was pondering an alliance of tribes to cope with the expansive colonists. According to an English observer, he visited the Montauks on eastern Long Island in 1642 and urged them to join with the Narragansett, much as the English settlers of Massachusetts and Connecticut had recently formed the United Colonies of New England. "So must we be one as they are," Miantonomi declared, "otherwise we shall all be gone shortly, for you know our fathers had plenty of deer and skins, our plains were full of deer, as also our woods, and of turkeys, and our coves full of fish and fowl. But these English have gotten our land, they with scythes cut down the grass, and with axes fell the trees."

Miantonomi never achieved such an alliance. In 1643 he was captured by Mohegans, who executed him at the bidding of leaders of the United Colonies. In the years ahead, Roger Williams and the Rhode Island settlers pursued an independent course, but they could do little to protect Narragansetts from the demands of the United Colonies, which forced tribal leaders to pay tribute in wampum or face attack. By 1660 Narragansett sachems were mortgaging their land to meet the tribute payments.

In southern New England as in Virginia, the loss of land coincided with an erosion of Algonquian spiritual traditions that was no less alarming to traditionalists. Roger Williams was unusual in that he preached to Narragansetts but refrained from formal mission work because he believed that it encouraged only superficial devotion rather than a "true turning to God." Elsewhere, English missionaries made intensive efforts to convert Algonquians to a new faith and a new way of life. Their task was made easier by the growing impression among native people that the English had great and mysterious powers at their disposal, as evidenced by the epidemics that accompanied their arrival and the devastation they inflicted with their firearms. An Algonquian named Wequash, who served as a guide for the English, told them that before the Pequot War, he had imagined their God as something small and annoying, like a mosquito or fly. After the massacre, however, he concluded that theirs was a "most dreadful God," and he converted to Christianity, if only to avoid God's wrath. Many other Algonquians began to heed Christian missionaries when they found that tribal shamans, or medicine men, were unable to protect them from European diseases and weapons.

The most ambitious English mission effort was led by the Reverend John Eliot, who learned to speak the language of the Massachusett people living near his home in Roxbury and later published a Bible in a phonetic version of their language that he devised. Eliot and his colleagues established a number of so-called praying towns, where Christian Indians could live and worship together, safe from the influences of traditionalists. The first praying town, Natick, was founded in 1651 on the banks of the Charles River, west of Boston. More than a dozen others were inaugurated in the area during the next two decades. But none matched Natick in design or scope. Under Eliot's direction, Natick's residents laid out an English-style town along three large streets, two on the north side of the river and a third on the south side, near the town's orchards and fields. They erected several buildings, including a two-story meeting house, and built an arched bridge across the Charles to connect the town with its plowed fields.

Aside from imparting Christianity, Eliot did all he could to promote English culture in the praying towns and discourage tribal practices. He ordered the construction of frame houses, although few were completed—they proved expensive to build and turned out to be colder in winter and hotter in summer than the wigwams Natick's residents preferred. Eliot required that residents wear "decent English apparel" and that the men crop their long hair, which signified manhood and accomplishment to Algonquians but represented mere vanity to Puritans. Other communal regulations prohibited polygamy, greasing the body with bear fat, "howling" during funerals, and the isolation of women during menstruation, which was punishable with a fine of 20 shillings. In addition, Eliot replaced clan and village leaders with elected officials, who served under the supervision of whites.

Residents of the praying towns had access to education and other benefits that were available to few non-Christian Indians. Students at the Natick school, for example, learned to read by mouthing a Christian catechism written down in their own tongue by John Eliot. Some Algonquian students went on to master English and even Latin, and several enrolled in a separate Indian College at Harvard, where the curriculum included Greek and Hebrew. The goal of the Puritan educators was to nurture a cadre of Christian Indians who would then instruct their own people in the faith. Some of the students did go on to become missionaries, but their influence was limited. By the 1670s, no more than 20 percent of the native population practiced Christianity, and less than 10 percent lived in praying towns. Most Algonquians residing in the area still occupied villages much like those of their ancestors and followed sachems who were linked by custom and descent to the chiefs of old. Indeed, mission-

In one of the fiercest assaults of King Philip's War, English forces attack Narragansetts holed up in the Great Swamp on December 19, 1675. Nearly 1,000 troops from the United Colonies overran the Narragansett fortifications. One colonist reported that the attackers killed several hundred warriors along with "their wives and children."

The seal of the Massachusetts Bay Colony features an Indian dressed in a fanciful girdle of leaves appealing to colonists to "Come over and help us." That injunction taken from the Bible reflected the belief of English missionaries that Algonquians were in dire need of their services.

ary efforts only incited some of the stronger and prouder tribal leaders against the colonists. Metacomet, who succeeded his father, Massasoit, as chief sachem of the Wampanoag, bluntly informed Eliot that he cared no more for the white man's gospel than he did for the button on Eliot's coat.

For Metacomet, known to the English as King Philip, the meddling of missionaries was just one of many grievances. Although his father had entered into an alliance with the Puritans in 1621 as an equal, Metacomet was treated as a subject of the colony. In 1665 he had to seek permission from authorities simply to buy a horse, a privilege the colonists denied to Indians. After rejecting his request, officials condescended to offer him a horse as a gift. More than once, Metacomet was summoned to court and required to pledge fidelity to the colony. But nothing angered him more than the use of alcohol and other inducements by colonists to wheedle land from Wampanoags, who found themselves increasingly outnumbered and outmaneuvered. By the 1670s, there were more than 50,000 colonists in New England, compared to about 15,000 Algonquians. As their domain dwindled, they not only had to toil for the colonists to support themselves but also had to obey English laws, including bans on hunting or fishing on the Sabbath and on using Indian medicines, many of which were more effective than English remedies.

In 1675 the simmering grievances boiled over. Colonists called the bitter conflict that ensued King Philip's War, and the Wampanoag chief was indeed the leader of the opposition. But Nipmucks in central Massachusetts were quick to join him in defying the English. And not long after the fighting began, the chief sachem of the Narragansett, Canonchet, enlisted reluctantly against the colonists as well after they tried to force him to surrender Wampanoags to whom he had offered protection. Canonchet refused, and many of his people fled to a fortified area in the Great Swamp, near Kingstown, where they were surrounded by English troops. In an assault grimly reminiscent of the Pequot massacre, the English slaughtered as many as 600 Narragansetts. Canonchet and a number of his warriors survived, however, and carried out retaliatory raids on towns in and around Rhode Island. Meanwhile, Eastern Abenakis in southeastern Maine—which settlers in Massachusetts regarded as an extension of their colony—had joined in King Philip's War after English sailors senselessly drowned the infant son of one of their chiefs in the Saco River.

The strength and scope of the resistance surprised the English, who saw a number of their towns destroyed in the early stages of the conflict.

But the colonists rallied and crushed the opposition, thanks to their superiority in numbers and weaponry as well as help from Mohawks—traditional foes of the Algonquians who attacked King Philip and his forces when they took refuge near Albany—and from Algonquian allies, including Mohegans and men from the praying towns. Those Christians fought for the English despite rank mistreatment by the colonists, who feared that the converts would turn against them and closed most of the praying towns. Some 500 Christian Indians were herded onto Deer Island in Massachusetts Bay, where many of them died of starvation before war's end.

Mashpee Wampanoags—some of them wearing unlikely wraps that may have been added to this anonymous painting for reasons of propriety after it was completed—gather under a tree to listen to a preacher thought to be Richard Bourne, the first missionary among the Mashpee. The Mashpee did not take part in King Philip's War, and Bourne subsequently helped them obtain a land title from the Plymouth Colony.

For the defiant Wampanoag and Narragansett, the conflict was catastrophic. King Philip was killed in battle, and thousands of his followers died in the fighting or perished from disease, hunger, or exposure when they were forced from their homes. Most of the survivors fled to remote spots to elude vengeful colonists or were sold into slavery like the vanquished Pequot. By the end of the war, the Narragansett population in Rhode Island had plummeted from more than 5,000 to fewer than 200, most of whom intermingled with Niantics on a small reservation they retained in the southeast corner of the colony. Chief Canonchet, who was captured and executed, made no appeal for mercy when he learned of his fate. "I like it well," he said. "I shall die before my heart is soft or I have said anything unworthy of myself."

The English victory was a hollow one for Roger Williams, who had preached tolerance for Indians and ended up commanding militia against them in a conflict that nearly obliterated the Narragansett. Nor was he the only leader whose high ideals foundered on the harsh realities of colonization. Another visionary who believed the Indians had a right to their land and livelihood was William Penn, founder of Pennsylvania. The wealthy son of an English admiral, Penn was a devout Quaker who visited the Delaware River valley in 1682 and established a colony of religious tolerance west of the Delaware. Penn and his Quaker followers were dedicated pacifists who hoped to bring people of differing cultures together in harmony.

The 1,000 or so Lenapes living in the area were at first suspicious of the Quakers. But when their chiefs met with Penn, they found that he spoke to them with respect rather than disdain and seemed genuinely concerned for their welfare. Like Roger Williams, he drew closer to tribal leaders by learning their language. "I have made it my business to understand it, that I might not want an interpreter on any occasion," he wrote. "And I must say, that I know not a language spoken in Europe that hath words of more sweetness in accent and emphasis than theirs."

Although Penn lived in Pennsylvania for only about four years, he governed the colony from abroad for more than three decades. During that time he tried to keep faith with the Lenape. He bought land from them, but on relatively generous terms and only after making it clear to tribal leaders what the consequences were. Penn's commissioners then sold parcels of the land they purchased to incoming settlers, reserving for Lenapes the village sites they already occupied. Over the years, however, colonists arrived who did not share Penn's ideals. Many of these newcomers were non-Quakers from various European countries who were attracted by the

In a painting by Edward Hicks, William Penn (center) concludes a peace treaty with Lenape chiefs at Shackamaxon in 1682—an accord commemorated by the wampum belt at right, given to Penn. Lenapes called him Miquon for the quill he used to sign accords. Penn praised the tribe's chiefs as shrewd negotiators who would not be fooled "in any treaty about a thing they understand."

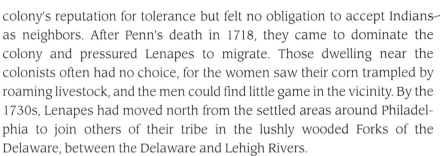

colony's reputation for tolerance but felt no obligation to accept Indians as neighbors. After Penn's death in 1718, they came to dominate the colony and pressured Lenapes to migrate. Those dwelling near the colonists often had no choice, for the women saw their corn trampled by roaming livestock, and the men could find little game in the vicinity. By the 1730s, Lenapes had moved north from the settled areas around Philadelphia to join others of their tribe in the lushly wooded Forks of the Delaware, between the Delaware and Lehigh Rivers.

Penn's own son, Thomas, played a leading role in defrauding Lenapes of that last major refuge in their ancestral homeland. In 1737 his agent produced a copy of a 50-year-old deed allegedly signed by his father and three Lenape chiefs that purported to cede to William Penn's heirs all land westward from a specified point in the Forks of the Delaware "as far as a man can go in one day and a half." Although the deed was of questionable authenticity (no original was ever produced), Lenapes grudgingly decided to honor it in the belief that the farthest a man could be expected to travel on foot through the forest in a day and a half—perhaps 30 miles or so—would still leave a significant area in their uncontested possession. But Thomas Penn and his brothers had already sold much of the area to settlers without informing the Lenape, and they now made sure of the outcome. With offers of land and money, they hired three fit men, who trained for nine days so they could cover as much ground as possible during the implementation of the Walking Purchase, as it became known. Thomas Penn also sent scouts into the woods to clear a path for the men.

On the day appointed to enact the Walking Purchase, the three men set out at a brisk jogging pace. Lenape observers complained, calling out to the men to walk, not run, but they hurried on. Two of the runners dropped out exhausted after the first day, but the third, Edward Marshall, covered almost 60 miles, enabling the Penns to claim nearly 1,200 square miles of Lenape land. Realizing that they had been cheated, Lenapes at first refused to leave. But under pressure from leaders of the still powerful Iroquois—who had forged a covenant with the English that gave them authority over weaker tribal groups—Lenapes embarked on a long and arduous migration that eventually carried many of them westward as far as Oklahoma.

Now English-speaking colonists were firmly in command of what had once been Algonquian country from Massachusetts southward. To the north, more and more English settlers were infiltrating the domain of the

Wabanaki and their French trading partners, triggering sharp clashes between the newcomers and French and Indian forces. In time, the English would prevail there as well, and Wabanakis would face the same choice as Algonquians elsewhere—migration or accommodation.

Those Algonquians who did not migrate to distant regions were relegated to small, scattered reservations or to the margins of English settlements. In either case, they found it difficult, if not impossible, to support themselves in the old ways. Many could no longer travel, for example, between their traditional hunting and farming sites. A number of their berry-picking fields and fishing spots were also off-limits. Some Lenapes remained behind in New Jersey and earned a meager living making baskets, mats, and brooms for sale to colonists. Other Algonquians on Long Island or coastal New England worked off debts by signing on with whaling ships. Their efforts sometimes made others rich, but few escaped poverty themselves. Meanwhile, in Rhode Island, one minister noted that the small number of Narragansetts still living there were "reduced to the condition of the laboring poor, without property, hewers of wood and drawers of water."

In Virginia, Powhatan men were still adept at hunting and fishing, but their skills were increasingly at the disposal of colonists. Powhatans had once made thorough use of the animals they killed, but now at least some men stalked deer for the trade value of the skins alone, "leaving the carcasses to perish in the woods," according to planter Robert Beverley.

Scenes like this one, showing the effects of a smallpox epidemic that swept from Connecticut to Maine in 1633 and killed thousands of Algonquians, were all too common during the colonial period. The heaviest losses occurred in the early years of contact, when European diseases reached virgin soil—communities with no acquired immunity. But epidemics continued to decimate Algonquian villages for generations to come.

Since the mid-1600s, Powhatans had been hunting wolves for bounties offered by the English and building fish weirs for payment that took various forms—one weir maker received shoes, stockings, and a pair of breeches. Even after Virginians learned to perform such tasks for themselves, Powhatan men were still sought after as guides, hunters, and fishermen.

Not all Algonquians were paid for their services, however. Some became the property of colonists and worked for them without wages. Throughout the colonies, a number of families owned Indian

A visitor attempts to persuade an Algonquian by offering him a bottle of liquor in an engraving with the ironic title "Manner of Instructing the Indians." Along the coast, whites used alcohol to induce Indians to enlist as whalers, among other purposes.

slaves—often captives taken in raids by European soldiers or by rival Indians who then sold them. And many colonists retained Indians as indentured servants, who toiled for their employers for a set number of years in exchange for food and shelter. Indentured servants could not be held legally without their consent—or in the case of children, the consent of their parents. But abuses were common. Algonquians did not always understand the terms of the indenture contracts they put their marks to. And parents were pressured to part with their children. In 17th-century Virginia, the African slave trade was still in its infancy and laborers were hard to come by. Colonists paid Powhatan parents to place their children in servitude. Only the neediest parents accepted the offer, and some colonists resorted to stealing Powhatan children. Even children obtained legally could be kept as servants for a decade or two; masters did not have to part with them until they were 24. And some servants were sold from one family to another like slaves.

On occasion, Algonquians did well as servants and succeeded on English terms. One Powhatan who did so, albeit modestly, was James Revell, who received that name from the hog farmer to whom he became indentured as a boy in 1667. By the age of 24, when his indenture ended, Revell had advanced to the position of overseer. One English boy who worked under him repeatedly refused to take orders from an "Indian dog," and Revell twice had to fight him to make him obey. Those incidents did not prevent Revell from successfully completing his indenture and start-ing his own hog farm. But a few decades later, in 1705, Virginia passed a law that grouped Indians with Africans as nonwhites and barred them from lifting a hand against any white person "on pain of getting thirty lashes on the bare back."

Many Indian servants and slaves ran away from their owners, often re-turning to their own people, who hid them. Some African slaves also sought refuge among various coastal tribes for a while. In Virginia, legisla-tors tried to discourage tribes from harboring runaways by offering Indians a bounty of a string of wampum as long as 20 arms for each Indian fugitive they returned alive and for each African they brought in dead or alive.

Most coastal Algonquians remained their own masters, but few could get by without selling their wares or skills to outsiders. Even if colonies set aside land for tribes on which they alone were permitted to farm and for-age, colonists often ignored those boundaries. In Maryland, for example, the assembly gave Nanticokes "free and uninterrupted possession" of a tract of land along the Nanticoke River in 1711, but settlers in the area en-croached on it repeatedly, cutting down vast numbers of trees for timber and refusing to reimburse the occupants. Some settlers simply squatted on the reservation or leased lots from impoverished Nanticokes without ever paying them. Legally, colonists had no claim to tribal land unless the rightful occupants decided to "desert and quit the same." Nanticokes com-plained to Maryland authorities that some settlers tried to make them desert by waiting until they were off on hunting expeditions and then set-ting fire to their lodges, leaving villagers "destitute of any cover." In 1767, recognizing that they would never be permitted to live undisturbed in Maryland, the 100 or so Nanticokes remaining on the reservation sold the land for $666.66 and moved northwest to join others of their tribe who had been offered protection by the Iroquois as a subsidiary family, or clan. Thus many Nanticokes ended up in New York or Canada.

The payment Algonquians received for their land or labor had a pro-found effect on their culture and made them all the more dependent on the colonists. From the start, the Indians had quickly incorporated Euro-pean goods into their way of life. Cast-iron pots, for example, reduced the reliance on the more fragile earthenware native women had long crafted. Bolts of European fabric, which could be made into clothing without first being dressed or tanned, took the place of deer and moose hides. Among Wabanakis, in particular, women often styled the new material in a tradi-tional manner, embroidering cloth with trade beads and ribbons in a way

Colonists lounge amid the vacant wigwams of an abandoned village in an area claimed by the Dutch. Europeans cited the migrations of Algonquians—whether in pursuit of subsistence or in flight from enemies or disease—as a reason for claiming their land.

that evoked some of their old designs. Other groups made do with the ready-made clothing traders provided. Among Lenapes, European shirts became popular. Men wore them loose and hanging to the knees.

Algonquians adapted many European items to their own purposes. Some men used Dutch stockings as tobacco pouches, for example, or wore steel hatchet blades on leather straps around their necks in place of their traditional copper gorgets. Iron hoes helped Algonquians work the soil more efficiently, and iron knives made it easier for them to carve canoes, bows, and snowshoes. With metal drills in place of stone ones, wampum makers became more productive. But the profits often went to others, as Europeans followed the example of tribes like the Pequot and Mahican and exacted wampum as tribute from groups along the coast. Much of the wampum was then offered to tribes in prime fur-bearing areas for beaver and other pelts that brought high prices in Europe.

The effect of the fur trade on Algonquian society was swift and far reaching. As Algonquian men turned from subsistence to commercial hunting, they depleted the populations of beaver and other sought-after species near the coast. As early as the mid-1600s, for example, beaver had become virtually extinct in the Lenape homeland. Hunters were forced to range farther inland. In some cases, entire Lenape villages dispersed, as women and children joined their husbands in the search for richer hunting grounds. Long before the bulk of the population migrated in the mid-1700s, pioneering Lenapes were heading west in small groups. With the breakup of villages came a weakening of clan ties and inherited lines of authority.

Few Algonquian communities that remained intact could claim to be self-sufficient. Women spent more time preparing hides for the market and less time planting and foraging for food. Some tribes became so engrossed in trapping and trading at the expense of other vital activities that they had to barter with Europeans or other Indians for provisions. Micmacs, who had traditionally spent much of the year on or near the coast gathering food from the waters, extended their inland hunting season for several months to pursue beaver and other small animals that yielded precious pelts but little meat. They relied on traders for provisions to see them through the winter. In some years, however, the demand for food exceeded the traders' supply, and Micmacs went hungry.

The fur trade also brought an escalation of tribal warfare, as groups competed for access to trapping grounds and trading posts. Early on, Abenakis fought with Micmacs for an advantage in the trade. Later the great challenge to Abenakis and Algonquians to their south came from

Algonquians pursue whales offshore while others carve up their catch on the beach in this 16th-century illustration. Companies usually provided the whalers with iron harpoons and other equipment. Some Algonquians amassed their own gear and went into business for themselves, only to falter in the face of sharp competition.

This whale-bone arrow point, found in Gouldsboro, Maine, was fashioned by Indians there some 2,000 years ago. Originally the coastal tribes harvested beached whales or those that became stranded in shallow waters.

ALGONQUIAN WHALERS

Long before colonists arrived, some coastal Algonquians were harvesting right whales that strayed close to their shores in winter, when the species ventured south from Arctic waters. By 1650 Europeans were hiring Indians to pursue those whales near the coast in open boats, armed with iron harpoons. The native whalers—including Montauks and Shinnecocks from Long Island and Wampanoags from Martha's Vineyard and Nantucket—towed their prey back to the shore for payment. Few earned much, however, because their employers deducted from their pay the value of goods extended to them on credit and of any lost or damaged gear. Many labored under debt from year to year.

Such exploitation only increased with the advent of deep-sea whaling in the early 1700s. Colonists were reluctant to embark on such long and dangerous voyages, and agents for whaling companies did all they could to procure able-bodied Algonquians by drawing them into debt. By 1730 three-fourths of the Indian whalers sailing from Nantucket were working to pay off their employers. A few Algonquians prospered in the whaling trade, but most had to content themselves with the intangible rewards of a hard job well done.

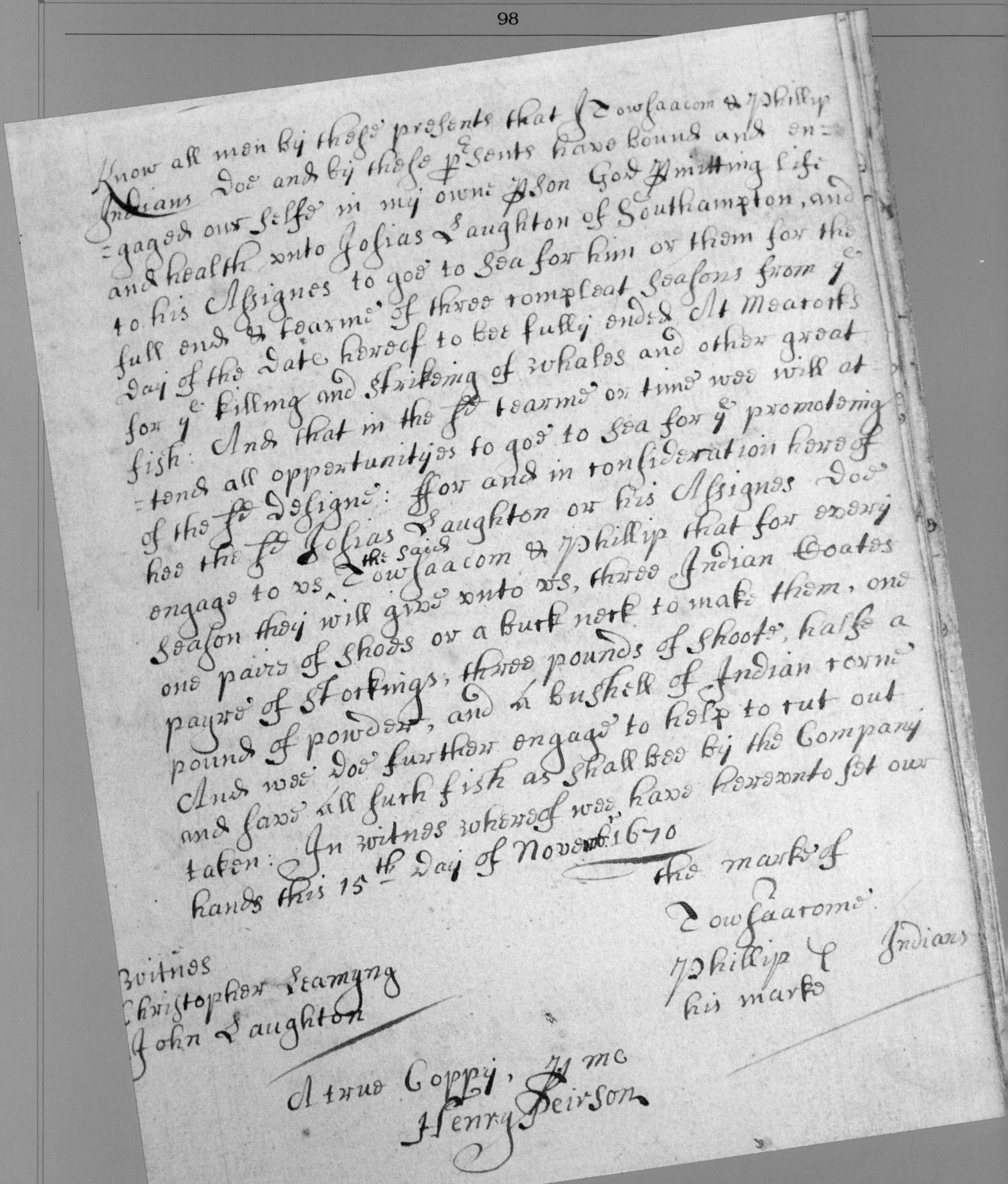

Know all men by these presents that I Cowsacom & Phillip
Indians Doe and by these presents have bound and en=
=gaged our selfe in my owne person God permitting life
and health unto Josias Laughton of Southampton, and
to his Assignes to goe to sea for him or them for the
full end & tearme of three compleat seasons from y
day of the date hereof to bee fully ended At Meacox's
for y killing and striking of whales and other great
fish: And that in the sd tearme or time wee will at=
=tend all opportunityes to goe to sea for y promoteing
of these sd designe: ffor and in consideration hereof
hee the sd Josias Laughton or his Assignes Doe
ngage to us the said Cowsacom & Phillip that for every
season they will give unto us, three Indian Coates
one pairs of shoes or a buck neck to make them, one
payre of stockings, three pounds of shoot, halfe a
pound of powder, and a bushell of Indian corne
And wee doe further engage to help to cut out
and save all such fish as shall bee by the Company
taken: In witnes whereof wee have hereunto set our
hands this 15th day of Novemb 1670

the mark of

Cowsaacome

Phillip   Indians
his marks

Witnes
Christopher Leamyng
John Laughton

A true Coppy, p me
Henry Peirson

On November 15, 1670, Shinnecock Indians named Towsacom and Phillip put their mark on this three-year contract for the "killing and striking of whales" along the coast and the rendering of the blubber onshore. In return, the two whalers were allotted clothing, shot and powder, and corn.

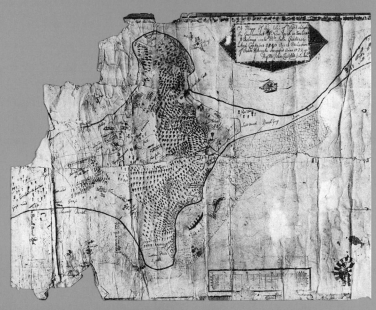

A 1722 map of Gardiners Island, off Long Island, shows six men hunting a whale in a craft of the sort companies provided to Algonquians who worked for them. Carved of cedar, each boat was 20 to 30 feet long and eight feet wide and carried a crew of four oarsmen, a helmsman, and a harpooner.

Of the many Wampanoags involved in deep-sea whaling, Amos Haskins of New Bedford, shown here in the mid-1800s, was one of the few who rose to become captain of a ship. In 1851, at the age of 35, he embarked on a whaling expedition in charge of a vessel named "Massasoit."

Iroquois warriors, who pushed eastward across Lake Champlain and the Hudson River in the hope of controlling the fur trade along those waterways. Europeans encouraged such intertribal disputes for reasons of their own. The French, for example, urged Abenakis to resist the Iroquois because the Iroquois were allied with the rival English and were raiding tribes around the Great Lakes that provided the French with their best pelts. Often Europeans bolstered their Indian allies with firearms, which greatly increased the toll of intertribal warfare and the demands for retribution. Roger Williams had observed that traditional Indian warfare in New England was "far less bloody and devouring than the cruel war of Europe." But once European weapons and trade goods were added to the mix, tribal wars became deadlier, ravaging villages—and generations of young men on whom the future depended.

Europeans brought further devastation to coastal tribes by introducing them to alcohol. Drunkenness did not come naturally to Algonquians. Early European witnesses were impressed by their moderation and self-discipline. In Virginia, for example, there were few reports of drunkenness among Powhatans before the late 1600s, when they had suffered severe blows to their morale. Even then, they tried to drink in a way that accorded with their traditions. As Robert Beverley observed, they imbibed solemnly, "as if it were part of their religion," much as they smoked their strong native tobacco to reach a state of spiritual intoxication. To prevent those who got drunk from coming to harm, one or two in each party would refrain and watch over the others. Nonetheless, drinking brought trouble and distress to Powhatans and other Algonquians, particularly when traders or land speculators encouraged the habit. Families went hungry when hunters bartered away a season's bounty of furs for a few bottles of rum, whiskey, or brandy. And communities were sometimes uprooted when tribal negotiators accepted the liquor that unscrupulous agents passed around to win concessions in treaty talks.

When colonists manipulated chiefs in this and other ways, they hurt Algonquians in spirit as well as substance by severing bonds of trust between the people and their leaders. In 1709 the colony of Rhode Island made the sachem of the Niantic—who served as chief over Narragansetts as well as members of his own tribe—the legal executor of their reservation. In practice, this meant that only the sachem himself, Ninigret II, and his family and heirs would benefit from the lease or sale of tribal lands. Other tribal members were permitted to fish, hunt, cut timber, and grow crops there, but they did not own any of the property. Nor could they pre-

This pipe tomahawk was presented to a tribal leader by an American negotiator. One side portrays an Indian with a tomahawk raised against an enemy. The other features an American eagle, signaling the new authority that Algonquians had to reckon with after the Revolutionary War.

vent the sachem or his heirs from selling large parcels to colonists, which many did to pay off personal debts.

Over the years, the Ninigret heirs came to live as landed gentry, with the same rights as other colonial freemen, including the privilege of voting. While other tribal members struggled to subsist, the sachem enjoyed the comfortable life of a wealthy plantation owner. A European visitor described the estate of George Ninigret, who presided as sachem from 1735 until his death in 1746. His manor house, called "King George's house or palace," was surrounded by more than 20,000 acres of fine level land, "upon which he has many tenants and has, of his own, a good stock of horses and other cattle. This king lives after English mode. His subjects have lost their own government policy and laws and are servants or vassals to the English here. His queen goes in a high modish dress in her silks, hoops, stays, and dresses like an English woman." When George Ninigret's son, Thomas, sold more tribal land to support this lavish lifestyle, his angry "subjects" secured a lawyer with the help of Samuel Niles—a Narragansett who served as a Baptist minister on the reservation—and opposed their chief in court. The court refused to intervene, and many on the reservation later sought refuge with other groups among the Oneida Iroquois, founding a Christian community at Brothertown, New York.

Reverend Niles, or Father Sam as he was called by his followers, was a product of the religious revival known as the Great Awakening that swept the colonies beginning in the 1730s. Adherents of this Protestant movement

As revealed by their costume, this 18th-century Abenaki couple at a Catholic mission village along the Saint Lawrence River in Quebec absorbed elements of French culture there. A number of Abenakis with ties to the French sought refuge in Quebec when their homeland was threatened, first by Iroquois warriors in the mid-1600s and later by English troops.

became known as the New Lights because they claimed to have discovered a new and certain path to salvation. In New England, Algonquians such as Niles were caught up in the revival because it allowed them to worship in a spirited and emotional way that conformed with their traditions. Niles, who could not read but learned much of the Bible by heart, was criticized by a rival minister for being guided less by scripture than by "feelings, impressions, visions, appearances, and directions of angels and of Christ himself in a visionary way." To Algonquians, however, visions were the essence of spirituality, and they expected as much from their holy men.

Niles, like most New Light preachers, respected tribal traditions that did not directly conflict with biblical teachings. With about 100 followers, he built a meeting house with an adjoining cemetery on the Rhode Island reservation and inaugurated an August Meeting there that harked back to the old Narragansett harvest ceremony. Even after the departure of many Christians on the reservation for Brothertown, the Freewill Baptist church Niles founded endured— as did the convivial August Meeting.

Maliseets gather by their canoes with a Catholic priest on their reservation at Kingsclear, New Brunswick, in the late 19th century to celebrate a religious holiday. The Maliseet were among the first Algonquians to be converted to Christianity, in the early 1600s, and their attachment to the faith grew stronger over the years.

Other Algonquian groups responded to overtures from Christian preachers during this period or grew more committed to beliefs introduced by earlier missionaries. In the north, Catholicism was now an integral part of tribal culture. Many Wabanakis attended morning and evening Mass, recited the catechism, and were baptized, married, and buried by Catholic priests. Indeed, the oldest Catholic cemetery in New England was established in 1688 among Penobscots on Indian Island, Maine. By the early 1700s, a Catholic priest could claim that the "whole Abenaki Nation is Christian and is very zealous in preserving its religion."

In the late 1730s, a group of Mahicans accepted the invitation of

missionary John Sergeant and settled the village of Stockbridge in western Massachusetts. There the church filled the traditional role of the chief's longhouse as the ceremonial focus of the community. Sergeant preached to the residents in the Mahican language, and some English families settled at Stockbridge to instruct Mahicans in crafts and serve as examples in other ways. Sergeant did not prohibit Mahicans from pursuing traditional subsistence activities, however. In late winter, for example, many residents went off to maple groves in the forest to harvest sugar, as they had in the past, leaving their children behind in a boarding school Sergeant established. Stockbridge served for a time as the site of Mahican councils, or the "fireplace of the nation," before colonists came to dominate the town.

In the meantime, other Mahicans and neighboring Algonquians were rallying around preachers of the Moravian Church—a group that was de-

voted to missionary work among tribal peoples. Moravians learned the languages of the Indians they ministered to and lived much as they did. Moravian mission communities were regarded by some outsiders as a threat, because temperance was firmly established there and the Indians could not be induced through liquor or other means to part with their land. Nor could they be enlisted to fight in colonial wars, because Moravians were pacifists. In New York, Moravian mission work among Indians was outlawed, and converts there migrated to Bethlehem, Pennsylvania, where they joined in a community with like-minded Lenapes.

Even Algonquians who did not formally convert reflected the influence of Christianity in their myths and legends. Powhatans, for example, no longer told of a single afterlife, where souls journeyed to the idyllic home of the Great Hare near the rising sun. They now spoke of another destination for wicked people after death, a place much like the Christian hell. One man described it as a "filthy stinking lake," where flames burned eternally and souls were tormented day and night by "furies in the shape of old women."

Colonists, for their part, had been influenced by Algonquians in ways that were no less remarkable. Throughout the region, settlers in remote areas wore moccasins, buckskins, and other worthy articles of native design; planted Indian corn and prepared it in Indian ways; traveled roads that followed ancient Algonquian paths; and hunted and fought with a cunning that few Europeans exhibited before they came in contact with Indians and learned from their example. Colonists had absorbed something from the Algonquians in spirit as well, as evidenced by their proud defiance of alien authority, culminating in the American Revolution. It was fitting that angry Massachusetts colonists dressed as Indians before they dumped tea into Boston Harbor in 1773 to protest English taxation, for King Philip and other native war leaders had given their ancestors cogent lessons in the meaning of resistance.

Unfortunately, few colonists recognized their debt to the indigenous people and cared whether their cultures survived. Most tribes lost far more than they gained from continued contact with Europeans. For staunch Algonquian traditionalists, the only solution was to spurn all whites, whether they came as enemies or as friends like the missionaries. In the 1760s, a Lenape prophet known as Neolin began preaching that all native peoples must return to the ways of their ancestors or face a sure and slow extinction. An impassioned and impressive speaker, Neolin said that the Great Spirit had warned him in a vision about the dangers of white culture. He urged Indians to give up European goods and live separately from the white man. "Can you not live without them?" he asked. "If you suffer the English among you, you are dead men. Sickness, smallpox, and their poison will destroy you entirely." Word of his warnings spread from one settlement to another.

But Neolin's message could not stem the tide of change sweeping over Algonquian lands. Nothing was as it had been. Now many Algonquians shared the dismay of a Wampanoag whose ancestral community on Martha's Vineyard had been devastated by smallpox. His people had once been led by wise men steeped in the lessons of the past, he lamented, "but they are dead, and their wisdom is buried with them, and now men live a giddy life, in ignorance, till they are white headed, and though ripe in years, yet then they go without wisdom to their graves." ✛

MICMAC QUILLWORK

To the French seamen who first encountered them about 1600, eastern Canada's Micmac Indians appeared wonderfully striking. Every item the coastal villagers wore, from their robes and moccasins to their necklaces and armbands, gleamed with brightly dyed porcupine quills—embroidered, woven, appliquéd, wrapped, and plaited into intricate designs "as lively as possibly may be," wrote an admiring sailor. Other of the Micmac's personal possessions were similarly beautiful, lavishly embellished by the tribe's women, who numbered among America's supreme quillwork artists. A century and a half later, the ravages of European contact had reduced those splendidly accoutered people to penury. They had become "intolerably ragged," according to one Englishman. To survive, the Micmac put their quillworking skills to commercial use. Concentrating on one relatively simple technique—appliquéing quilled patterns on birch bark—they crafted colorful souvenirs for curio-hungry Europeans. The market for Micmac quillwork reached its peak in the ornament-mad Victorian era. Small lidded boxes were the most popular items, but the ingenious quillworkers also created hundreds of other birch-bark commodities: razor cases, pincushions, tea cozies, napkin rings, wall hangings, tabletops—and such novelties as the receptacle shown here, designed to collect the combed hair of a Victorian lady.

OPEN-TOPPED, WALL-HUNG HAIR COMBINGS BOX

EARLY-20TH-CENTURY BOX LID

BOX WITH TRADITIONAL STARFISH DESIGN

**ROUND BIRCH-BARK BOX
WITH CHEVRON DESIGN**

OPEN-TOPPED RETICULE

**SMALL TRUNK-SHAPED
BOX, CIRCA 1850**

LETTER RACK WITH SLOTS FOR ENVELOPES

PINCUSHION WITH BEADED RIBBON EDGE

RIBBON-SEAMED TEA COZY

OCTAGONAL DECORATIVE PLATE WITH BEADS

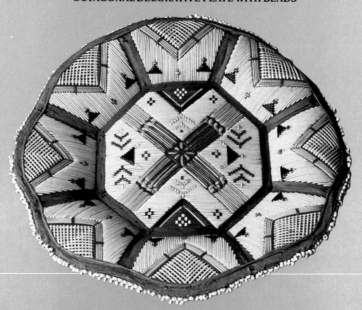

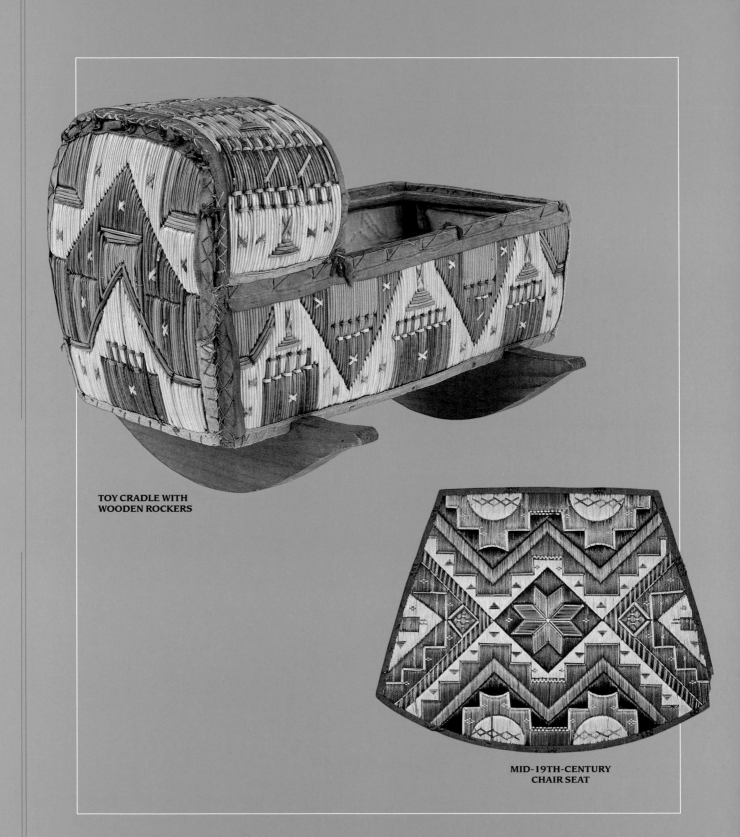

**TOY CRADLE WITH
WOODEN ROCKERS**

**MID-19TH-CENTURY
CHAIR SEAT**

**CHAIR WITH QUILLED
BACK PANEL AND SEAT**

SACRED SMOKE RISING

For the eastern Algonquians, as for most Native Americans, tobacco is a sacred substance that some believe originated from the bones of a mythical first mother. Down through the years, the plant has played an important role in Indian ritual. Before embarking on any venture, Algonquians traditionally made an offering of tobacco, sometimes as the crumbled leaf but most often smoked. The rising smoke is visible evidence of man's desire for contact with the spirit powers above and within the natural world. The gesture signifies commitment and makes a request for support. In relationships with fellow humans, the sharing of a pipe suggests the trust and intimacy of a common purpose.

Although the origin of tobacco rituals is uncertain, such practices were widespread at the time of European contact. The Indians also took the herb medicinally as well as for relaxation. In the evenings, Algonquian men sat down together to enjoy a smoke. Indeed, tobacco was so central to life that a man always carried a pipe and pouch with him. The oldest pipes were made of clay or soapstone and sometimes had animal or spirit effigies carved on the bowls. Others had reed stems up to six feet long.

The eastern Algonquians grew a hardy species of tobacco known scientifically as *Nicotiana rustica*. The men cultivated the plants in special gardens set apart from the food crops tended by the women. For a milder smoke, they mixed the crushed tobacco leaves with the leaves of other plants, such as sumac, and the inner bark of dogwood and cedar trees. They called the blend kinnikinnick, an Algonquian word meaning "that which is mixed." Each tribe had its own formula.

Many Algonquians still use tobacco to bring them into harmony with nature. When Henry Bess (Thunder Bird), ceremonial chief of Long Island's Shinnecock Indians, died in 1989, the men of his family performed a tobacco ritual and buried him with a pipe in his hand filled with fresh kinnikinnick.

This spirit face once formed part of a pipe bowl made by the Lenape, later known as the Delaware. When the bowl broke, the owner preserved the effigy, presumably because he believed that it was imbued with power.

An 18th-century German watercolor illustrates "Nicotiana rustica," Indian tobacco, with its characteristic yellow flowers.

Tishcohan, a Lenape chief, sat for this 1735 portrait wearing a tobacco pouch of chipmunk skin around his neck.

PIPES OF THE ANCIENTS

This tubular stone pipe and pebble filter date to 450 BC. The two were found in a hilltop grave on the New Jersey bank of the Delaware River.

The face of a spirit— probably Mesingw, the Keeper of Game—appears on the bowl of this clay pipe dating from about 1600.

A bear climbing a tree enlivens this stone pipe bowl from coastal Massachusetts. The opening for the stem is on the bear's back and passes through its hind legs.

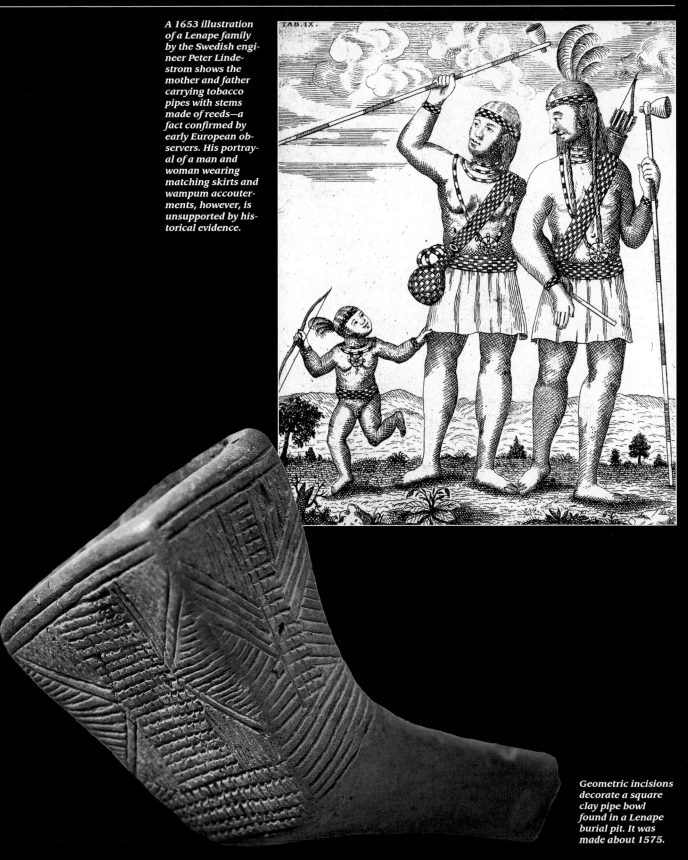

A 1653 illustration of a Lenape family by the Swedish engineer Peter Lindestrom shows the mother and father carrying tobacco pipes with stems made of reeds—a fact confirmed by early European observers. His portrayal of a man and woman wearing matching skirts and wampum accouterments, however, is unsupported by historical evidence.

TAB.IX.

Geometric incisions decorate a square clay pipe bowl found in a Lenape burial pit. It was made about 1575.

THE ENDURING VESSEL

In this woodcut, Wampanoag chief Massasoit offers the peace pipe to Pilgrim governor John Carver. The 1621 ceremony marked the treaty between the two groups that lasted until after Massasoit's death in 1661.

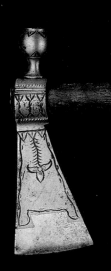

A bear, a beaver, and an otter encircle the stone bowl of this 19th-century Micmac pipe. Blue and green beads are wrapped around the wooden stem.

The bird effigies carved on this pewter trade pipe are thought to be the swallow-tailed kite, a type of falcon.

This British-made combination implement, common at the time of the American Revolution, could be used as both tomahawk and pipe. The weapon's wooden handle served as the stem of the pipe.

William Brown, an Oklahoma Delaware, carries a pipe tomahawk in a 1909 photograph. The Delaware maintained their special relationship with tobacco after migrating west from their eastern homelands.

Pigeon and other bird feathers, colored thread, and beads decorate this calico smoking bag, made about 1850 by a Micmac Indian in Newfoundland. The bag has three pockets to hold a pipe, tobacco, and fire-starting materials.

REAFFIRMING OLD WAYS

The broad leaves of this Indian tobacco plant on the Shinnecock Reservation on Long Island are almost ready for harvesting. Commercial cigarette tobacco comes from a taller, leafier variety of plant.

Lamont Smith (left), a Shinnecock Indian, shows a friend how he dries tobacco from his garden in wooden trays. The dried leaves will be used ceremonially.

This modern tobacco pouch, which is adorned with embroidery, beads, and leather fringe, was made by John Kenney, a Shinnecock craftsman.

Herbalist Nora Thompson Dean, an Oklahoma Delaware, places an offering of tobacco and cedar leaves in a bucket of burning coal at the 1977 dedication of the Delaware Indian Resource Center at Ward Pound Ridge Reservation, Cross River, New York.

THE CEREMONY OF TOBACCO

A Plains tribe gave this contemporary pipe to Charles C. Clark IV, assistant chief of the Nanticoke. "The bowl of red pipestone," Clark says, "represents the earth, and the wooden stem all the good things that grow on the earth."

Charles Clark leads the pipe ceremony during the 1994 Nanticoke Powwow held in Millsboro, Delaware. He implores the Four Directions, Mother Earth, and Father Sky to share their strength with the assembled people.

3

THE SEARCH FOR RESTITUTION

A Delaware chieftain named Nonondagumun sat for this portrait by George Catlin in 1832. "No other tribe on the continent has been so much moved," the painter remarked of the Delaware, "or fought their way so desperately, as they have honourably and bravely contended for every foot of ground they have passed over."

Of all the coastal tribes displaced during colonial times, none ventured farther from their homeland than the Lenape. After losing what remained of their ancestral territory as a result of the Walking Purchase, most Lenapes had resettled by the early 1740s along the Susquehanna River in Pennsylvania. This area, then at the frontier of colonial America, was under the control of the Iroquois. Before consenting to share their land, the Iroquois struck a tenuous agreement with the Lenape that the two groups would, in the words of the Iroquois, act as man and woman. That is, the Lenape would remain close to home and refrain from competing with the Iroquois in exchange for sanctuary. With much reluctance, the Lenape submitted to the conditions of the Iroquois. After all, they were refugees, having been driven from their homeland by the implacable advance of white settlements. And the Susquehanna region made a more than satisfactory home. Its vast forests teemed with wildlife, and the fertile river valley guaranteed bountiful crops.

But the gracious surroundings were not enough to keep the Lenape from chafing under the domination of the Iroquois. Within 10 years, many of them, led by the forceful leader Shingas, went west again, crossing the mountains to the Allegheny and Ohio River valleys. There, away from the influence of both English and Iroquois, Lenapes reasserted their communal identity. To signal their independence, they decided that henceforth they would be a nation of people known as the Delaware, that they would follow the counsel of their own elders and warriors, and that they would forcibly resist English intruders.

Shingas saw a golden opportunity to strike at the encroaching English when they became embroiled in the French and Indian War in 1754. Shingas allied his people with the French and launched devastating raids against English colonists. In a few years, Delaware war parties killed hundreds of settlers and succeeded in driving the English frontier back to eastern Pennsylvania. Iroquois leaders who had sided with the English asked Shingas and his followers to cease their raids. The response of the Delaware was swift and uncompromising: "We are men, and are determined not to be ruled any longer by you as women, and we are determined to cut off all the English, except those that may make their escape from us in ships; so say no more to us on that head, lest we cut off your private parts, and make women of you, as you have done of us."

Such defiant words reflected the deep indignation of Algonquians who had been deprived not only of territory but also of self-respect. The Delaware went to unusual lengths in an effort to recoup those losses. Other eastern Algonquians stayed put and grudgingly accepted the limits imposed on them by authorities. Some intermarried with non-Indians or Indians of other groups until their tribal affiliations were largely obscured. In time, however, many of the coastal tribes regrouped and worked to reclaim rights or property that had been wrested from them. In that sense, the journey of the Delaware anticipated the search of other Algonquians for restitution, whether in some distant country or in the land of their ancestors.

For all their determination, Shingas and his followers were soon forced to give ground. In 1756 the Pennsylvania and New Jersey colonies

Arrows mark the route of the Delaware's forced migration from their eastern homeland to Oklahoma, half a continent away. The majority of the tribe's members moved west gradually, arriving in eastern Oklahoma in 1868, but some factions settled along the way in Ontario and Wisconsin. The so-called Absentee Delawares, a group that split off from the main body of the tribe about 1789, headed for Texas but settled finally in western Oklahoma.

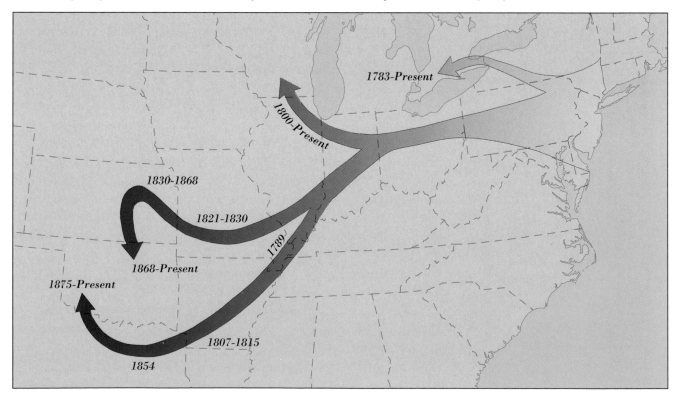

Wearing a cape of stitched ribbonwork reminiscent of Great Lakes Indian design, an Oklahoma Delaware woman poses for a photographer in the 19th century. Delaware crafts and customs often revealed the influence of the tribes who lived along the route taken by the migrants.

responded to the raids by declaring war on the Delaware, offering bounties for prisoners or scalps. A 300-man colonial force marched west and on September 8 attacked a major village of the Delaware—Kittanning—on the Allegheny River northeast of the French stronghold at Fort Duquesne. They killed many of the warriors, including a leading war chief, destroyed a large cache of supplies, and burned the village. The survivors dispersed to villages farther west, in order to put Fort Duquesne between them and any future English expeditions. But in 1758, the exhausted and outnumbered French forces abandoned the fort and the Ohio Valley, and retreated to Canada. Shingas yielded power to his brother Beaver, who served as a peace chief and negotiated the best possible terms with the English. Colonial emissaries assured the Delaware that British forces would withdraw and that settlers would not be allowed west of the Alleghenies. But British soldiers stayed on at the garrison they renamed Fort Pitt.

Almost immediately, in defiance of the peace treaty, a tide of white settlers began to spread westward from Fort Pitt. Angered by this betrayal and inspired by the prophet Neolin to resist white men's ways, the Delaware joined in a general uprising by refugee tribes, organized in 1763 by the Ottawa chief Pontiac. But neither the Delaware nor their allies could sustain the effort without access to trade goods such as weapons and ammunition, and their inevitable surrender came in 1765. The peace terms imposed on the Delaware required that they forfeit all claims to land ownership and abandon their opposition to white settlement west of the Alleghenies.

Nonetheless, the Delaware found refuge in the Ohio country on land granted them by the Wyandot—a Huron group. There a chief called Netawatwees, or Newcomer, had recently established a settlement of about 700 people known as Newcomerstown, whose log cabins and bark huts stretched for a mile and a half along the Tuscarawas River. Other Delaware communities sprouted up in the area after Pontiac's War. The villagers resumed their accustomed annual round of gardening, hunting, and trapping. But they had become dependent on white traders for such necessities as iron tools, cloth, firearms, gunpowder, and lead shot. In order to secure the pelts they needed for trade, the men ransacked their new homeland for beaver, deer, bear, and raccoon, killing thousands of animals and depleting the populations.

In the wake of the traders came Moravian missionaries, who continued in Ohio the work they had begun among Lenapes who had remained behind in the East. The Moravians converted hundreds of Delawares, moving them to mission towns, where they were encouraged to lead lives of industriousness, modesty, and pacifism. The mission towns were built at least 10 miles away from other Delaware villages to keep the converted from the unconverted. When American colonists went to war against their mother country in 1775, the Moravians and their converts hoped to avoid the conflict. Some Delawares favored the rebellious colonists, while others were inclined to oppose them in the hope of stemming the tide of settlement, as English authorities had recently promised.

When the Americans prepared to march an army through Delaware territory to attack the English at Detroit, they contrived to buy assurance

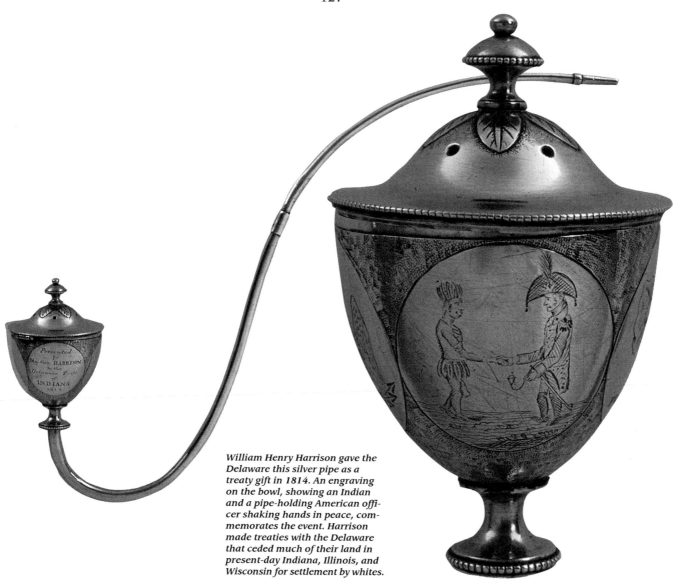

William Henry Harrison gave the Delaware this silver pipe as a treaty gift in 1814. An engraving on the bowl, showing an Indian and a pipe-holding American officer shaking hands in peace, commemorates the event. Harrison made treaties with the Delaware that ceded much of their land in present-day Indiana, Illinois, and Wisconsin for settlement by whites.

of safe passage from the tribe. On September 17, 1778, after receiving $10,000 worth of trade goods and promises of continuing assistance, Delaware chiefs signed the first Indian treaty executed by the fledgling United States of America. In the treaty, the Delaware agreed to provide guides, food, and horses to the American troops. For their part, the Americans consented to build a fort and protect the Delaware from retaliation by the British and their Indian allies. Remarkably, the treaty also proposed the creation of a 14th state for Indians who remained friendly to the United States, with the Delaware at their head. But the American army bound for Detroit was rebuffed before it reached that goal and had to retreat, leaving the Delaware to fend for themselves. Delaware war leaders who had never trusted the Americans persuaded most of the tribe to change sides, and led warriors out to attack American settlements.

The Americans wasted no time in responding. In the spring of 1781, American troops destroyed Coshocton, which had surpassed Newcom-

erstown as the principal Delaware settlement on the Tuscarawas. The following year, a band of 160 Pennsylvania volunteers marched to the Ohio country to punish the Delaware for continued depredations on the frontier. They found Coshocton in rubble and the other Delaware villages in the area deserted, except for one—the Moravian mission town of Gnadenhutten, founded 10 years before. The Delawares there had remained neutral and participated in no raids. Nevertheless, the vengeful Pennsylvanians rounded up all 90 men, women, and children living in the town and slaughtered them. The killers were never punished, and their action, one of the worst atrocities of the Revolutionary War, all but destroyed American credibility among the Delaware.

A carved face of Mesingw, the powerful Delaware forest spirit, adorns the center post of a ceremonial Xingwikaon, or Big House (inset). The seasonal Big House Ceremony lasted for up to 12 consecutive days and nights and served to give thanks for the harvest and other blessings from the Creator.

After the Revolutionary War ended in 1783, the American government concluded a treaty with various groups of Indians living in the Ohio country. Under its terms, the Delaware were forced to cede their abandoned villages and lands along the Tuscarawas and nearby Muskingum Rivers in eastern Ohio. Most of the villagers had taken refuge in central and western Ohio and hoped to remain there. But the white frontier continued to advance, prompting fresh conflict between Indians and settlers. Delawares

Images of Mesingw adorn ceremonial drumsticks, shown here with a sacred water drum. Placed so that they always look upon the drummer, the faces were carved in accordance with the instructions said to have been given to the Delaware by the spirit himself.

joined forces with Shawnees and Miamis in the area to raid the settlers and defy American troops dispatched to defend them. For a while, the allied tribes prevailed. But in 1794, Major General "Mad" Anthony Wayne, with an army of federal troops, marched into Ohio and defeated the Indians at the Battle of Fallen Timbers. The resulting treaty dislodged the Delaware once more. With the permission of the Miami, they settled on the West Fork of the White River in what is now Indiana.

By this time, the main body of the Delaware had been reduced in number by the departure of splinter groups. One party had set out for the west as early as 1789 and settled in Missouri. And a group of Moravian converts had since emigrated to Canada in the hope of escaping the relentless conflict along the frontier. For the majority of the tribe that moved to Indiana, life proved difficult. Although the land along the river was fertile, many men resisted farming and the harvests were not enough to sustain the people. With no war to employ the men as soldiers and guides, and fur no longer in great demand, the tribe became impoverished both materially and spiritually.

Some Delawares found solace by reviving ancient beliefs, ceremonies, feasts, and dances. A female prophet named Beate realized that the people were too poor to provide for the traditional round of feast days. She initiated, instead, a single annual celebration, held for 12 days in October, that came to be known as the Big House Ceremony. The festival centered on a structure resembling the traditional longhouse of the Delaware. This Big House—built without the use of any foreign materials such as iron nails or glass windows—depicted the Delaware universe. Its center post symbolized the tree that rose to heaven from the back of the great turtle that supported the earth. Sacred masks were carved on either side of the center post and on 10 posts around the perimeter of the dance floor, representing 12 points on the White Path that souls traveled on their way to the next life. Dancers joined symbolically in that great journey by circling the center post each evening in a counterclockwise direction. On the 12th night, the dancers completed their passage and celebrated as if they were in paradise.

Amid this revival of native spirituality, some Delawares responded enthusiastically to the preaching of a charismatic Shawnee prophet by the name of Tenskwatawa, brother of the

war chief Tecumseh. Tenskwatawa's message, which urged a return to ancestral customs as well as a total renunciation of alcohol, appealed to those members of the tribe who were searching for guidance. His opposition to any dealings with the Americans was so great, however, that he accused those inclined toward peaceful coexistence of practicing witchcraft. Several of the accused, including a Delaware chief, were tortured and burned to death by Tenskwatawa's followers.

The killings antagonized many Delawares and kept them from joining a burgeoning resistance movement formed by Tenskwatawa and Tecumseh, whose followers were defeated by American troops in 1811 along the Tippecanoe River in Indiana but continued their resistance by supporting the British in the War of 1812. The Delaware, under a forceful new leader

The design of this Delaware coat, fashioned from buckskin and ornamented with silk ribbon and glass beads, was influenced by the style of the Plains Indians who originally inhabited the Oklahoma Territory where the Delaware and other eastern tribes settled.

An Episcopal missionary oversees the progress of her Delaware charges during a sewing class in Oklahoma sometime around 1898. Most missionaries believed that assimilation into white culture was crucial to the Indians' acceptance of Christian beliefs.

known as William Anderson, remained neutral in the conflict despite the appeals of their benefactors, the Miami, who urged them to assist the British. William Henry Harrison, governor of the Indiana Territory and superintendent of Indian affairs there as well as commander of U.S. troops in the region, said of the Delaware: "This tribe is entirely to be depended upon. Their fidelity to the United States is unquestionable."

The tribe's neutral stance during the War of 1812 did not protect them from further disruption. Afterward, Indiana became a state and tens of thousands of American settlers streamed westward, forcing the tribe to negotiate yet another treaty with the government. In exchange for a lump-sum payment of roughly $13,000 for their land rights plus a perpetual annuity of about $4,000, they gave up their Indiana land and agreed to move west of the Mississippi. In 1820 more than 1,300 Delawares headed out, most of them on horseback. As they made their way across Illinois, they were plagued by horse thieves and swarms of insects, ran short of supplies, and fell hungry and sick. To make matters worse, they had no clear destination, because the government had not decided just where on the west side of the Mississippi they were to settle.

The groups camped on the river's west bank for months before being directed to a tract of marshy land in southwestern Missouri. When they arrived, the Delaware began building a village, but the site was prone to flooding and game was scarce. Moreover, there were rival claims for the area not only from other Indian tribes such as the Osage but also from American settlers who were squatting there. Chief Anderson demanded a better place for his people to live, and in 1829, the United States agreed to relocate the Delaware to Kansas. The new site of nearly two million acres was located at the forks of the Kansas and Missouri Rivers. This time, Anderson drove a harder bargain. He asked for and received better compensation and more plentiful supplies—not only for the journey but also for a year thereafter—and arranged for prior inspection of the new lands by members of the tribe. He insisted on horses, teams of oxen, wagons, and other equipment in order to reach Kansas and begin farming, which he believed was crucial to future success. "It will not be long," he predicted, "until there is no more game. Then our young hunters will lay by their guns and go to work."

In Kansas, the Delaware enjoyed a measure of stability and prosperity for a few decades. They built villages with schools, converted to Christianity in significant numbers, and took up farming. They won renown as breeders of livestock and as hunters and guides for expeditions, such as those of John Frémont and John James Audubon. When the Civil War erupted in 1861, Delawares in Kansas sided with the North. Of 247 Delaware males over 18 years of age living in the state, 170 volunteered for service in the Union army. "This is probably the largest ratio of volunteers furnished for the war," noted Indian agent Fielding Johnson. In his view, it demonstrated a "patriotism unequaled in the history of the country." Their dedication went unrewarded, however. In response to pressure from white settlers and the powerful railroads, the federal government imposed new treaty terms that required the Delaware to sell their land in Kansas. With part of the proceeds, the Delaware purchased 160,000 acres from the Cherokee in an area along the Caney River in northeast Oklahoma, or the Indian Territory, as it was then known.

Once more the Delaware set out on a perilous migration. They gave up their houses, fields, friends, schools, and churches, and all the household goods they could not carry with them. They straggled southward from December 1867 through the summer of 1868, receiving no protection or assistance along the way. A number of them died. Those who endured suffered an indignity that was all too familiar to Delawares with long memories: dependency on another tribe. As part of the land deal, they became citizens of—and in many ways subject to—the Cherokee Nation. Cherokees who were already living along the Caney River when the

Members of a Delaware family tend their animals outside their Oklahoma log farmhouse in a photograph dated June 28, 1901. Having settled into more sedentary lives by the time they reached Oklahoma, most Delaware Indians favored log-constructed homes over their traditional bark lodges.

Delaware arrived were allowed to remain there, and the immigrants had to find places among them. In some cases, Delawares cleared land, only to discover that Cherokees had already claimed it. Cherokee chiefs spoke for the Delaware and tried persistently to get them to share their treasury.

After more than a century of struggle, the Delaware were still living as exiles, without a true homeland that they could call their own. But the memory of all that their ancestors had endured and fought for inspired them in the years ahead to cling to their cultural identity. They remained an original people—a legacy of which they could never be deprived.

T he Delaware were not the only eastern Algonquian group to migrate in large numbers. In northern New England, decades of conflict with the English and their Iroquois allies had induced many Wabanakis to resettle in Canada by the middle of the 18th century. During the French and Indian War, a number of those refugees fought for the French and saw their adopted homeland invaded by English forces, who destroyed the native village of Saint Francis near the Saint Lawrence River in 1759. At the end of the war, English colonists celebrated their victory by flooding into Vermont, New Hampshire, and Maine in a rush known as the "great swarming time." Their burgeoning settlements displaced most of the Indians who had not already departed. But a few tribal groups remained in the area in significant numbers—notably the Penobscot and Passamaquoddy in Maine.

When the American Revolution broke out, the rebellious colonists courted the strategically placed Penobscot and Passamaquoddy, taking steps to halt encroachment on Indian lands. Both tribes agreed to side with the Americans in the conflict, joining Benedict Arnold's expedition against British forces in Quebec and helping to fight off British attacks in eastern Maine. Despite the momentary gratitude of the fledgling nation, which was expressed in a personal message of friendship to the Passamaquoddies from George Washington, the fruits of victory were bitter for the Indians. The state of Massachusetts—of which Maine was then part—pressed them to cede a large portion of their land. Under severe economic constraints, the Passamaquoddies acquiesced in 1794 and sold more than one million acres to the state. Many Passamaquoddies were confined to a small reservation located at Pleasant Point, Maine. Shortly thereafter, the Penobscot yielded 200,000 acres of their land in exchange for annual payments of cloth, rum, corn, and shot.

Fire engulfs a Catholic mission, as a French missionary, Father Sebastian Rasles, prepares to receive a mortal blow in this lithograph depicting a raid by the English and their Indian allies. The priest, a Jesuit, spent 30 years with the Abenaki in Maine before suffering his violent death in 1724.

In 1818, to raise money for the Penobscot and avoid selling off more land, Chief John Attean attempted to sell timber felled on tribal lands. Massachusetts denied the right of the Penobscot to sell the timber and forced the sale of the land itself. A few years later, the new state of Maine declared the Indians to be government wards and appropriated most of their remaining land. By the middle of the 19th century, the Penobscot retained only a few islands in the Penobscot River, with Old Town on Indian Island their principal community.

As their domain dwindled, the subsistence pattern of Wabanakis changed dramatically. American farmers fenced off farmland and loggers decimated the forests, driving away the large game animals that had long been a major source of food for members of the tribe. At the same time, the demand for furs declined, depriving the Wabanaki of their principal source of trade goods. Some of the men sought additional income as lumbermen, millworkers, or farm hands. Both men and women discovered a market among settlers and tourists for various handicrafts, including birch-bark canoes, carved bone knives, shell jewelry, buckskin clothing, and, especially, fine baskets made from ash-wood splints.

Always excellent watermen, Penobscots now were pressed into service as guides for American hunters and sportsmen. One such escort was John Attean's son, Chief Joseph Attean, who earned mention in Henry David Thoreau's book, *The Maine Woods,* after guiding Thoreau on a tour of the back country in the 1850s. Described by the author as a "good-looking Indian, 24 years old, apparently of unmixed blood, short and stout, with a broad face and reddish complexion," Attean hunted moose on the trip while Thoreau watched with rapt attention. Thoreau thrilled to the chase, entranced with how Attean traveled "lightly and gracefully, stealing through the bushes with the least possible noise, in a way which no white man does." But he was less than delighted with the actual killing, calling it a "tragical business." For Wabanakis, however, the real pity was that few of their men could still support their families with such skills—and that even their chiefs now had to hire out their services.

A gunpowder flask, thought to be the property of the great Penobscot chief Joseph Orono, features an incised drawing of a large three-masted ship. Orono, a staunch ally of the American rebels, was so impressed by the French frigates he saw anchored in Boston Harbor during the Revolutionary War that friends nicknamed him Big Ship.

The process of assimilation had begun earlier in southern New England. There most Algonquians had adopted the English language, dress, and style of housing by the beginning of the 19th century. The Pequot, Narragansett, and Wampanoag had suffered crushing defeats in earlier times and had dwindled to the point that they were largely invisible to the outside world. Herman Melville, in his novel *Moby Dick,* published in 1851, named Captain Ahab's vessel after the Pequot—a tribe "as extinct as the ancient Medes," in the words of the narrator. In fact, a small number of Pequots still lived in Connecticut and environs, descendants of those who had returned from exile after the Pequot War. But the surviving members of the tribe were so isolated, or so acculturated, that whites hardly noticed them.

A Penobscot boatman ferries a passenger to Indian Island in Maine's Penobscot River in a photograph taken about 1900. A series of treaties following the Revolutionary War deprived the Indians in Maine of much of their land, and by the 1850s, most Penobscots lived on Indian Island, isolated from the white communities that surrounded them.

Even as they seemed to blend in, the Algonquians of southern New England adhered to certain traditions. Most men continued to resist the idea of farming as women's work and tried almost anything else to earn their living. Narragansetts became adept at stonemasonry. Wampanoags and Pequots continued to enlist as crewmen on whaling ships. Members of various tribes rented their land to whites, clear-cut it and sold the wood, or manufactured handy items for sale such as brooms, brushes, and baskets. Men and women alike found satisfaction in such craftsmanship through gathering the materials, designing the products, and teaching the work to others and thus preserving part of the culture. But the peddling of the valued items was degrading at times, and the returns scant.

Algonquian communities that remained intact, like the Wampanoag reserves of Gay Head on Martha's Vineyard and Mashpee on Cape Cod, came under intense pressure from outsiders eager to exploit Indian land and labor. The Mashpee, who had been guided by missionaries since the 1640s, successfully petitioned English authorities for limited self-rule in

Three women of the Maliseet tribe of the Maine-New Brunswick border area peddle a variety of handcrafted wares including brooms, baskets, and bark containers in this watercolor from about 1840. When they were no longer able to make a living by trapping and hunting, many tribes began selling their traditional crafts to whites.

the mid-18th century, only to lose that privilege after the American Revolution. Keeping the Mashpee powerless suited their white neighbors, who were jealously eyeing the timber on the Mashpee "plantation," as it was known. "Wood at many of the other towns on the Cape is very scarce," noted a missionary in 1795. "At Mashpee it is plenty. Great numbers have located themselves near this plantation and are eagerly anticipating opportunities to come into the possession of this Indian interest."

At Gay Head, it was the services of sea-wise Wampanoags that whites coveted. Recruiters stopped at nothing to fill their rolls for the lengthy whaling voyages that replaced the shorter coastal expeditions of earlier times. Captains in search of crew members, a visitor to Gay Head reported, would indulge in a "sort of crimping, in which liquor, goods, and fair words are plied, till the Indian gets into debt, and gives his consent." Using liquor as an inducement promoted alcoholism and made it that much harder for the whalers to escape indebtedness. "An Indian that goes to sea is ruined," the visitor concluded, "and his family is ruined with him."

Once on the whaling ships, Wampanoags worked alongside men of other races. Indeed, many Algonquians of southern New England mingled with other peoples. The Mashpee had a longstanding policy of offering refuge to groups that were not welcome elsewhere, having informed the Massachusetts Bay Colony in the mid-1700s that they were prepared to "receive any other Indians or mulattoes to share with us in our privileges and properties." The invitation specifically did not extend to "any English or white man." By the late 1700s, a missionary in Mashpee counted about 400 people there "who are greatly and variously mixed," with "only 25 males and about 110 females who are truly originals and not mixed." One successful product of such intermingling was Paul Cuffe, the son of a West African slave who had purchased his freedom from his Quaker master and married a Wampanoag woman. Paul Cuffe shipped out as a whaler in 1775 at age 16 and went on to become the owner of his own small fleet of vessels. He, too, married a Wampanoag woman and honored both his African and Indian heritage by forcefully opposing slavery.

Some Narragansetts living off the reservation in Rhode Island also worked and intermarried with black slaves on plantations in the southern part of the state before slavery was abolished there in 1784. Not all

This woven covered basket was created by contemporary Passamaquoddy artisan Irene Newell. The value of such handcrafted works has increased because of the mounting respect for native art forms among collectors.

tribes welcomed the offspring of such mixed marriages, because they feared being stigmatized by whites as "colored." When Narragansetts moved from the reservation at Charlestown to live among the Oneida at Brothertown, New York, they were informed by Oneidas that none of the land was available to those who were "descended from or have intermixed with Negroes or mulattoes." Such racial concerns among Indians were heightened by the actions of white authorities. In 1792 the Rhode Island legislature gave adult male reservation dwellers the right to vote for their own council, so long as they were not born of a "Negro woman."

Some Algonquians refused on principle to discriminate in this manner. William Apess, a Pequot who was born into poverty in 1798 and grew up to become a Methodist missionary, wrote in 1833 that it was "folly to think that the white man, being one in 15 or 16, are the only beloved images of God." Presaging the civil rights movement of the 20th century, Apess spoke out in his sermons and writings against the injustices visited on all "colored people." His travels took him to Mashpee, where he agitated for a return to self-government and boldly defied whites who were trespassing on Mashpee property. In July 1833, he and a group of followers confronted two white men who were hauling away wood from Mashpee territory and forced them to retreat empty-handed. Apess was arrested and sentenced to a fine and 30 days in jail for his part in this Mashpee Revolt, as it became known. But he gained sympathy for his cause, and in 1834, the Mashpee Wampanoags won an unprecedented measure of autonomy from the Commonwealth of Massachusetts. Apess deemed his jail term worthwhile. "In my mind, it was no punishment at all," he said. "I am yet to learn what punishment can dismay a man conscious of his own innocence."

The victory was short-lived. In the 1870s, Massachusetts joined Rhode Island and Connecticut in seeking to sell off Indian lands and disband the tribes that were living there. Massachusetts, for example, converted the reservations at Mashpee and Gay Head into towns. Much of the land at Mashpee that had been held in common by the community was sold to outsiders. Rhode Island proposed to buy the Charlestown reservation and auction it off to the public. Each tribal member would receive a

A silhouette of whaling captain Paul Cuffe appears above a ship symbolically spanning the distance between the palm-treed shore of Africa and the rocky coast of New England. The son of a freed black slave and a Wampanoag woman, Cuffe succeeded in an industry where many Indians met misery. An ardent abolitionist, he once used his ship to repatriate 38 freed slaves to the African colony of Sierra Leone.

share of the purchase price and become a citizen of the state. But Narragansetts suspected that if they were looked upon as "colored" people, their rights would be severely limited. Joshua H. Noka of the Narragansett tribal council said that "for a colored man to be a citizen, he will remain about the same as at the present time." No such person, he said, should expect to be elected president or even selected for a jury, "but if you have got a cesspool to dig out, put him in there."

In the end, the Narragansett tribal council had little choice but to sell what remained of their land. Proceeds from the 922 acres brought each of the 324 tribal members $15.43. By 1883 the 250-year relationship between the Narragansett and the white settlers of Rhode Island had been terminated. In the words of an official report, the "name of the Narragansett tribe now passes from the statute books of the state." Gideon Adams, the last man to head the Narragansett council, declared that "our tribe now has no legal existence, and no person can be found to represent the Indian race. The change is so great, I feel sorry to think of it."

For southern Algonquians, living in an area where slavery endured until the Civil War and segregation persisted long after, the issue of race proved especially troublesome. Most Nanticokes had left Maryland and Delaware by the middle of the 18th century, some carrying with them the bones of their ancestors to be reburied in distant lands. A small group of Nanticokes went west and settled with the Delaware. But most took refuge with the Iroquois, joined them in opposing the Americans during the Revolutionary War, and fled to Canada in the bitter aftermath. "We are driven back until we can retreat no further," lamented one Nanticoke exile. "A little longer and the white man shall cease to pursue us, for we shall cease to exist."

Those few Nanticokes who remained in their coastal homeland faced adversity of a different sort. For a while, they kept to themselves, frequenting swamps, islands, and remote necks of land too barren or inaccessible to attract white settlers. Soon, however, even those spots were intruded upon, and Nanticokes could no longer avoid contact. They began to work as tenant farmers for white landowners, saving as much as they could from their wages to purchase firm deeds to their own property. A community bearing the name Nanticoke emerged on the Indian River in Sussex County, Delaware. But the hopes of the residents to succeed on white terms were undermined by punitive race laws enacted in the wake of the

PASSAMAQUODDY WOMAN, 19TH CENTURY

WARREN CUFFEE, SHINNECOCK, UNION CIVIL WAR VETERAN

slave rebellion led by Nat Turner in Virginia in 1831. Those laws were aimed at blacks and mulattoes—forbidding them from possessing weapons, preaching sermons, or even assembling without supervision—but whites increasingly looked upon Indians as "colored" people and subjected them to similar treatment.

Among those who felt the sting was a Nanticoke named Levin Sockum, who had started out as an obscure laborer and tenant farmer and advanced to become a storekeeper, landowner, and one of the wealthiest men in Sussex County. In 1856 he was charged with breaking a state law that made it illegal for anyone to sell gunpowder to a black or mulatto. The gunpowder had been purchased by another prosperous Nanticoke named Isaac Harman, who was married to Sockum's daughter. The defense attorney wrote later of Harman that "of all the men concerned in the trial he was the most perfect type of the pure Caucasian, and by odds the handsomest man in the courtroom, yet he was alleged to be a mulatto."

Securing testimony about Harman's ancestry proved difficult, but finally the prosecutor brought to the stand an elderly Indian woman related to Harman—the last of the Nanticokes in Delaware who could speak her native language. The woman, Lydia Clark, asserted at the trial that one of Harman's grandfathers had been a black slave. Sockum was found guilty and fined. Nanticokes asserted ever after that Lydia Clark had been induced to testify against Sockum and Harman by the white family that

The early photographic portraits shown here and on the following pages offer a range of the Algonquian-speaking peoples inhabiting the Atlantic Coast from the dense forests of Maine to the tidewater region of Virginia. As their features and clothing attest, these people represent societies that evolved under the influence of the various cultures that impinged on their homeland.

DORCAS HONORABLE, NANTUCKET WAMPANOAG, CIRCA 1840   LOUIS SOCKALEXIS, PENOBSCOT BALLPLAYER

pressed the charges. When Clark died less than a year later, her tombstone—reportedly provided by that same family—was inscribed with the tribute that she had been a "person of truth and a witness against the arrogant Negroes that assumed to be what they were not."

The practice of discriminating against Indians as "colored" people continued long after the abolition of slavery. In 1875 Delaware passed an act taxing all "colored persons" $.30 for every $100 worth of their property to fund segregated schools for nonwhites. This meant that Nanticokes in the state would no longer be able to operate their own informal educational system, involving instruction at home and occasional class meetings in a church or barn—a tradition that helped preserve their distinct cultural identity. Determined to fight back, Nanticokes organized and hired a lawyer and pressed for exemption from the tax law with the proviso that they would provide their own schooling, as in the past. After a six-year campaign, the legislature authorized the "Indian River School District for a Certain Class of Colored Persons."

Although the Nanticoke won the right to educate their own children, building two one-room schools on donated land, they were still subject to racial discrimination. Demanding formal acknowledgment as Indians, they appealed to the assembly again in 1903. During the next session, the legislators conceded their existence, proclaiming that the "descendants of the Nanticoke Indians shall hereafter be recognized as such within the

EUNICE MAUWEE, PEQUOT WOMAN, CIRCA 1858

MICMAC WOMAN, CIRCA 1851

state of Delaware." Some years later, the state tried to force the placement of non-Indians in the Nanticoke schools. The Nanticoke again sought legal recourse, and in 1922, the state of Delaware formally incorporated them, with their chief serving as the body's chief executive officer.

In Virginia, meanwhile, the remaining Powhatans had been laboring under a similar burden of discrimination. By the late 18th century, decades of intermarriage there had blurred the racial lines between blacks, whites, and Indians. In 1785 Virginia conceded as much by easing its legal definition of mulatto from one-eighth African ancestry (or one African great-grandparent) to one-fourth African ancestry (or one African grandparent). This seemingly made it easier for Indians to avoid the strictures that applied to blacks and mulattoes. But at the same time, white planters were becoming increasingly concerned that Indians were intermingling with free blacks, who were portrayed as unruly and potentially rebellious.

In 1784 planters on Virginia's Eastern Shore accused a band of Accomacs there known as Gingaskins of allowing their land to be used as an "asylum for free Negroes and other disorderly persons" and thus creating a "den of thieves and nuisance to the neighborhood." In the planters' view, the Indians were not making proper use of the land because of their "fondness for fishing, fowling, and hunting, the natural insolence of their disposition, and their natural disinclination to agriculture." In fact, many women on the reservation still cultivated corn and other crops as their an-

PAMUNKEY FAMILY PORTRAIT, 1899

cestors had. A few years later, the planters alleged that Gingaskins had intermarried with blacks to such an extent that there were "not more than three or four of the genuine Indians" left on the reservation. They petitioned the Virginia General Assembly to expel the free blacks, sell the reservation, and use the proceeds to support only those Indians who "appear to be genuine descendants of the tribe."

The General Assembly resisted the demands of the Eastern Shore planters, agreeing only to oversight of the reservation by trustees. But in 1812, the trustees pressured the Gingaskins into accepting the allotment of their reservation, and the following year, Virginia enacted the first such law in the United States. The reservation was divided into plots that were duly apportioned to the 27 "true" Gingaskin adults, who could then sell them or continue to live on them as taxpayers. For nearly two decades, two-thirds of the Gingaskins held on to their land. Then, within a few months of the Nat Turner rebellion and the ensuing hysteria, almost all of the remaining plots were sold under duress. The remaining Gingaskin people stayed on to become squatters on land the white farmers did not want, and eventually merged into the local black population.

Other tribal groups suffered as well in the aftermath of the Nat Turner rebellion. Virginia passed laws in the 1830s that denied nonwhites the right to possess a weapon, conduct or address a meeting, learn to read, or be tried by a jury. As in other states, these laws applied to blacks and mulattoes, but they affected Indians who were suspected of being at least one-fourth black. Powhatans faced repression if they were identified as free "colored" persons—and confinement if they were mistaken for fugitive slaves. They could be jailed if they neglected to carry a certificate confirming that they were free, and even sold into slavery if no one appeared to testify on their behalf.

Residents of the two remaining Powhatan reservations in Virginia—the Pamunkey and Mattaponi—struggled to maintain their identity as Indians and thus preserve their territory and their prerogatives, including the right to bear arms, guaranteed under a treaty they reached with Virginia in 1677 that granted them hunting privileges. In 1843 white neighbors of the Pamunkey petitioned the assembly to terminate the reservation on the dubious grounds that all the residents were mulattoes, possessing "one-fourth or more of Negro blood." Pamunkeys responded with petitions of their own and managed to retain their reservation, but they came under further pressure in the years ahead. In 1857 neighboring whites confiscated their firearms. Tribal representatives protested the action to Virginia's governor, who affirmed that the Indians had the right to bear arms. "They tell me their mode of living is by hunting," he wrote, "and to deprive them of their firearms is in effect to drive them away from their lands, which the laws most emphatically forbid."

Alienated from their white neighbors, hardly any Powhatans enlisted with the Confederacy during the Civil War, and a few signed up with the Union army. After the war, some Powhatans took advantage of the opportunities afforded by Reconstruction and served in public office. But white segregationists soon regained control of the state, and Indians there again found themselves subject to discrimination as nonwhites. In 1900 state legislators mandated separate public facilities for whites and "colored" people. In 1924 Virginia passed the Racial Integrity Law that defined as white only those people without a trace of non-Caucasian blood—the single exception being those who were at most one-sixteenth Indian. That exception was inserted for the benefit of those Virginians who claimed descent from Pocahontas and planter John Rolfe. A number of them were from influential families, and they wanted to be able to boast of their distant link to the Powhatan "princess" without having to use separate bathrooms and other inferior facilities designated for nonwhites.

By the early 20th century, the enduring members of the eastern Algonquian tribes could count their very survival as an accomplishment. Some

EVOLUTIONS
IN STYLE

By the 1800s, the ready availability of European trade goods had altered the dress of most Algonquian peoples. The women found textile cloth and thread easier to work with than the customary hides, sinews, and moose hair. And glass beads, silk ribbons, and colored embroidery threads gave the artisans versatile new materials with which to practice their decorative needlework. In particular, Wabanakis such as Canada's Micmac and the Penobscot of Maine—examples of whose artistry are pictured on these pages—created extraordinary new fashions by blending traditional and European materials and motifs.

MICMAC WOMAN'S
PEAKED CAP

Christina Morris, a noted 19th-century Micmac quill- and beadworker, wears a typical woman's peaked cap, a style also worn by the Maliseet, Passama-quoddy, and Penob-scot. The distinctive conical shape of the headpieces may have been inspired by Basque caps that were brought to Canada by French sailors about 1600.

MICMAC WOMAN'S
BEADED VEST

HEAVILY BEADED
PENOBSCOT
BABY CAP

MICMAC MOCCASINS
BEADED WITH LINES AND
STYLIZED FLOWERS

Mercy Nonsuch, a Niantic woman, holds a bag beaded in a European-inspired flower design. Beadworkers also employed traditional motifs such as borders of parallel lines, as on the moccasins at bottom opposite.

19TH-CENTURY CLOTH AND RIBBON POUCH

PENOBSCOT MAN'S COLLAR
BEADED IN A SCROLL-AND-
FLOWER MOTIF

19TH-CENTURY
PENOBSCOT MAN'S
EPAULET

Dressed in full cere-
monial garb in the
early 20th century,
Penobscot governor
Peter Nicola wears
a pair of beaded
epaulets and a col-
lar worked in a
European-derived
floral pattern.

MICMAC MAN'S GREAT-COAT, CIRCA 1840

Gabe Paul, a Penobscot, wears a traditional man's eared headdress and a beaded greatcoat. The French and English gave their Indian allies plain military greatcoats, which the women decorated with heavy beading that sometimes added as much as 30 pounds to the garment's weight.

Western Abenaki craftsman Joseph Paul Denis, photographed in 1923, displays some of his handmade birch-bark canoe models. Although they were only small-scale representations, the canoes were constructed in the traditional Abenaki fashion.

of them remained on reservations that had been sadly whittled down, while others lived on the fringes of white society and were scarcely recognized as Indians. Yet their tribal identity had not been extinguished.

The Penobscot, isolated as they were on Indian Island in Maine and the few other areas they inhabited, still retained vestiges of their old habits and culture. In recent years, however, they had been attending schools where only English was spoken, working outside their communities, and intermarrying with other groups. In 1907 anthropologist Frank Speck seized what he thought might be the last opportunity to study a vanishing culture. Hoping to document the "thought and action of old Indians drawn from experience and memory going back to their own youth and childhood," Speck conducted a rigorous, 11-year study of the Penobscot people. He observed and recorded the "still distinctly Indian" ways of the approximately 400 tribal members in Maine, documenting their artistic traditions, social relationships, and religious ceremonies.

Speck accompanied Penobscot families who struggled to support themselves in the traditional manner, moving from fishing camps along the coast in the summer to interior hunting grounds in the fall before returning to Indian Island for the winter months. He witnessed, among other customs, the Penobscot hunter's age-old method of luring a bull moose to a stream by calling the animal with a bark horn, then pouring water from the horn to mimic the inviting sounds of a prospective mate.

Speck returned to Maine in 1936 to reappraise the lifestyle of the people he had come to know. He saw new ways displacing the old, as in the case of 85-year-old Louis Nicholas, whom Speck had known as a strong and vigorous hunter and guide but who was now cadging pennies from tourists by performing traditional dances and ancient prayers in the street. Speck saw tears in the old man's eyes and understood that he was praying to be taken soon to heaven to join his long-dead friends. Speck feared that much of his repertoire would die with him and called it the "end of Penobscot musical history."

Speck also found that some tribal values had endured "beneath the surface of commercialism," that the "clangor of the mills across the river and the hum of traffic . . . have not deafened the ears of all Maine Indians to the pleasant whisperings of evergreens or to the thrilling bellow of the moose in fall." He also noted hopefully that Penobscots were as adventurous as ever, citing one man from Indian Island who had "accompanied a geodetic survey party to Alaska as woodsman, been 140 feet below water

Young Franklin Delano Roosevelt paddles a canoe fashioned by Passamaquoddy craftsman Tomah Joseph. During the 20th century, the seasonal round for the Passamaquoddies included serving as guides and outfitters to vacationing sportsmen.

As part of a ceremony held at the state capitol in Richmond in 1985, Pamunkey Indians present Virginia governor Charles Robb with a deer as tribute in accordance with a long-ago treaty provision.

in a caisson building the Bath Bridge, defied the 'bends,' scrambled along four-inch steel girders 200 feet above the river as a riveter, spent four years with the Canadian forces on the German front . . . and is now awaiting a date to guide sportsmen on the Allagash and Saint John Rivers."

By the 1920s, coastal Algonquians were caught up in the pan-Indian movement that was bringing native peoples closer together throughout North America. Tribes in the northeast formed the Indian Council of New England and came up with a motto that resonated deeply with groups like the Narragansett and Pequot who had been all but forgotten: "We are still here." In Virginia about the same time, nonreservation tribes formally incorporated themselves and joined the Pamunkey and Mattaponi in what they called the Powhatan Confederacy. Members of the confederacy gathered at powwows with Algonquians from Maryland and Delaware to celebrate their common heritage and discuss their grievances. Although Indians around the nation were declared U.S. citizens in 1924 and granted the right to vote, those in Virginia and many other states were prevented from going to the polls for years to come. Not until after World War II did the federal government insist that Indians—who had been subject to the draft during the war like other citizens—be allowed to vote in presidential elections. That privilege was not extended to Indians in Maine until 1954.

Gains in civil rights for Indians led to heightened activism, and a number of coastal Algonquian tribes mounted legal efforts to recover lost territory. At first the justice system appeared to offer them little recourse. State courts refused to hear such land claims on the grounds that they were federal matters. For their part, the federal courts adhered to a late-19th-century ruling that tribal land disputes in the 13 original states were outside the jurisdiction of the federal government. But a surprising decision by the U.S. Supreme Court in 1974 on behalf of the Oneida Iroquois of New York upheld the 1790 Indian Trade and Intercourse Act—forbidding disposal of Indian land by anything other than a federal law—and opened the floodgates for tribal land claims. Since most Algonquian lands had been appropriated by state governments without regard to the 1790 law, the tribes now had legal grounds to recover their land. The court cases were long and arduous, but in the end, several tribes that had lost much if not all of their territory scored heartening victories. The state of Rhode Island, for example, restored to the Narragansett approximately 2,000 acres in the Charlestown area. Other settlements awarded land—or monetary compensation—to the Pamunkey, the Pequot, the Gay Head Wampanoag, and the Penobscot and Passamaquoddy.

Tribes that accepted money as part of the settlement faced the challenge of investing it wisely and fairly. The Penobscot and Passamaquoddy, for example, pressed claims for 12.5 million acres, or nearly two-thirds of the state of Maine. Landowners there grew so alarmed that the federal government stepped in and offered the tribes a landmark settlement by which the tribes renounced their claims in exchange for $81.5 million, part of which was set aside to purchase 300,000 acres of land for the tribes. Of the remainder, the Passamaquoddy used a share to buy a cement factory, a radio station, and a blueberry farm. They turned the cement plant into a lucrative business and resold it at an enormous profit. Not all the tribe's ventures proved so successful, however, and some Passamaquoddies complained that the investments had failed to boost employment within the community. In 1994 half of the adults on the Pleasant

Point Reservation were unemployed. Some residents felt that the windfall had done little to improve their prospects.

The Penobscot also invested proceeds from the settlement—in real-estate development, mobile-home sales, and audio-cassette manufacturing. They built an ice hockey arena on Indian Island to rent to area schools and colleges and named it after Louis Sockalexis, the Penobscot major-leaguer who played for the baseball team that became the Cleveland Indians. None of the ventures turned a profit, however, and in 1982, the state shut down their one moneymaking enterprise, a high-stakes bingo

Fancy-dancing men step in time to a drumbeat (above) and children wear their finest regalia (inset) at the 1994 Nanticoke Powwow held near Millsboro, Delaware. After centuries of assimilation into white society, many eastern tribes have adopted the traditional clothing of the Plains Indians for ceremonies to show their pride as members of the larger pan-Indian community.

operation. By 1990 per capita income on the reservation was 30 percent below that of the surrounding area, and many tribal members were once again dependent on welfare. But there was hope for the future. The Penobscot were taking advantage of the educational opportunities afforded them and could claim the same percentage of high-school graduates as neighboring communities. And in the 1990s, Maine agreed to a smaller-stakes bingo operation on Indian Island. The ice hockey arena became the Sockalexis Bingo Palace.

Not all tribal groups were successful in pressing their land claims. The Mashpee Wampanoag, for example, filed suit in the 1970s against the town of Mashpee and the state of Massachusetts in federal court, seeking to recover some of the land taken from them when Massachusetts converted their reservation into a town. Since the land had been disposed of without a federal treaty, the Mashpee were confident of the outcome. But despite testimony from anthropologists and other expert witnesses that supported their tribal status as Wampanoags, a jury found that they were not entitled to restitution because they were not a tribe in the strict terms set out by the presiding judge in his instructions to them. The Gay Head Wampanoag later succeeded in gaining federal recognition as a subtribe, and the Mashpee have appealed for similar recognition in the hope of reversing the court decision.

For Connecticut's Pequot, the struggle for restitution yielded astonishing rewards. In 1973, after the death of Elizabeth George Plouffe, the last Pequot Indian occupying the tribe's tiny reservation at Mashantucket in Connecticut, the state was ready to convert the reservation into a park. But Plouffe had urged her grandson, Richard "Skip" Hayward, to "hold on to the land." Hayward, who as a boy had lived with his grandmother on the reservation in a house without running water or electricity while his father was at sea, had been inspired by the lively tales she told him of Pequot trials and triumphs. To honor his grandmother's request, Hayward began a relentless struggle to pull the Pequot together and keep their heritage alive. He moved back to the reservation after she died and asked every Pequot he knew to join him. At first, only a few

did so, but they succeeded in preserving the reservation and then launched a campaign to expand it.

Under Hayward's leadership, the tribe filed suit in 1976 against the state of Connecticut to recover 800 acres of land. The Pequot also sought state and federal recognition as a tribe and tried to make the reservation self-sufficient. Hayward tried various ventures, from pig farming to a hydroponic greenhouse, without much success. In 1983 a breakthrough occurred. The Pequot won state and federal recognition as a tribe. With the acknowledgment came a $900,000 land claim settlement and eligibility for government assistance for housing, jobs, and social services.

By this time, the reservation had a population of 50 Pequots—each certified to have had an ancestor listed on the tribal census of 1900—living in 15 homes built with low-interest federal loans. Still searching for economic independence, Hayward proposed building a large bingo hall. The Pequot at first voted the proposal down, fearing public criticism. But Hayward persisted, and narrowly won a second referendum. After obtaining venture capital from the Penobscot, the Pequot began a profitable bingo operation in 1986.

Hayward did not stop there. He secured the backing of a Malaysian investor and, after overcoming the objections of neighboring residents and the state of Connecticut, built a resort complex that consisted of two gambling casinos, a luxury hotel, and a shopping mall. The complex, called Foxwoods, opened in February 1992 with a payroll of more than 9,000 employees and began pumping $1 billion a year in profits into the bank account of the Pequot tribe. Before long, tribal members were enjoying luxury housing, medical care, job training, day care for the young, and nursing care for the elderly. Each member also received an annual profit-sharing bonus from the revenues of the casinos.

Gamblers check off their cards at the bingo hall at Foxwoods casino on the Pequot Reservation in Connecticut. The most successful high-stakes bingo game on the East Coast, the hall has hosted packed houses every day since it opened, generating enormous wealth for the once struggling tribe.

Joey Carter, who serves as tribal spokes-man, poses in front of the sign welcoming gamblers to the Pequot's casino complex. The casino's incredible success enables the tribe to provide comprehensive social services for its nearly 250 members.

Wisely, the Pequot did not count on gambling casinos for all of their future revenue. They reinvested much of their profit in real estate and other business ventures—as well as in the education of their children, who received full private-school and college scholarships. Moreover, they have shared their bounty with other Indians, offering assistance to tribes around the country eager to start their own commercial operations.

Few Algonquians have been as fortunate as the Pequot, and some have chosen not to follow in their footsteps. Residents of the Mattaponi and Pamunkey Reservations in Virginia, for example, have resisted the lure of gambling. They and other Powhatan groups have relied on small government grants and on the contributions of their own members to fund the establishment of tribal centers.

In one way or another, the spirit of renewal has touched all Algonquians. And many people outside of tribal circles have come to admire them for their remarkable persistence in the face of seemingly overwhelming obstacles. Algonquians of the East Coast are at last gaining recognition as the land's true pioneers—the original people who prepared the ground and planted the seeds from which great things emerged. ◆

A FEAST FOR THE WAMPANOAG

Wampanoag elder Russell Peters and his grandson Steven use a canoe to gather seaweed from the shore of Popponesset Bay in preparation for the feast called Appanaug.

Earth, fire, water, and food from the sea come together in the Appanaug (literally, "seafood cooking"), a traditional feast celebrated by the Mashpee Wampanoag Indians on Massachusetts's historic Cape Cod. No one knows when the Indians first learned how to combine hot rocks and a type of seaweed known as rockweed to create a natural oven for steaming shellfish, vegetables, and other foods. But according to Wampanoag tradition, the feast was part of tribal life long before 1620, when the ancestors first welcomed the Pilgrims.

Mashpee Wampanoags customarily hold their bakes to honor one of the tribe's members or in conjunction with a special occasion, such as a seasonal thanksgiving. The Indians still harvest a great deal of the seafood themselves from the waters of their homeland, although they sometimes purchase certain items such as sausage and onions at local markets. Here and on the following pages, Russell Peters shares the secrets of a Mashpee Wampanoag "bakemaster" with his 12-year-old grandson Steven.

Steaming hot lobsters and cheesecloth bags filled with corn, clams, onions, and sausage sit atop a bed of seaweed in a bake pit that has just been opened.

GATHERING THE ESSENTIALS

Peters shows his grandson and two young friends the clams he has just dug from the shores of Popponesset Bay. At low tide, telltale air holes in the sand at the water's edge reveal the location of the buried clam beds.

Steven and his friends wade into the waters of the bay to "scratch" for quahogs. The children twist their bare feet into the muddy bottom of the bay until they feel a hard object. Rocks encountered this way are thrown away toward the deep water.

Ralph Hendricks, a Wampanoag fisherman, holds a mesh bag filled with his catch—sea scallops harvested from the waters off Cape Cod.

Peters and Steven fill their canoe with the bake's vital component—rockweed. The aquatic plant will provide a bed for the food to rest in as it cooks. The rockweed's bubble-like cavities contain enough seawater to supply a steady, salty steam.

STOKING THE OVEN

After digging a shallow circular pit, Peters directs his grandson to line it with the rocks that will give off the heat required for the bake (above). After the pit is properly lined, wood is piled atop the rocks for the fire (right). The blaze must be strong enough to heat the rocks to a white-hot glow.

Peters and Steven watch the fire die down (top). At the right moment, they will rake out the hot ashes, leaving only the rocks at the bottom of the bake pit. Rockweed is then quickly placed over the hot stones (above). It not only provides moisture for a cooking steam but also adds a smoky, earthy flavoring to the food.

BAKING AND TALETELLING

Fresh lobsters crown a mound of locally gathered food atop the sizzling, steamy rockweed (above). The cheesecloth bags holding other foods are a modern innovation that allows for easier handling.

After covering the bake pit with a tarp to hold in the briny steam, Steven and his friends admire their handiwork (left). The pit will stay covered for 60 to 90 minutes to ensure that all of the food is thoroughly cooked.

A lull in the baking activities provides time for elder members of the Wampanoag community to visit with the youngsters and amuse and instruct them with stories.

SHARING THE BOUNTY

Grandfather and grandson share the duties of serving lobsters to the guests (right). A hearty bowl of quahog chowder has sharpened their appetites for the feast that awaits them.

Peters serves himself after all the guests have received their portions. The rockweed will continue to steam for hours, keeping the leftover food warm and moist.

Two Wampanoag children savor the delicious rewards of the bakemaster's labor. In time, their children and grandchildren will enjoy the ancient tradition of the Appanaug.

ACKNOWLEDGMENTS

The editors wish to thank the following individuals and institutions for their valuable assistance:

In Canada:
New Brunswick—Peter Larocque, Regina Mantin, New Brunswick Museum, Saint John. Nova Scotia—Ruth Whitehead, Nova Scotia Museum, Halifax. Quebec—Margery Toner, Canadian Museum of Civilization, Hull.

In Denmark:
Copenhagen—Berete Due, National Museum of Denmark.

In the United States:
 Delaware: Millsboro—Charles C. Clark IV.
 Maine: Bar Harbor—Rebecca Cole-Will, Anne Stocking, Robert Abbe Museum.
 New Jersey: Trenton—Lorraine Williams, New Jersey State Museum.
 New York: Ronkonkoma—Chepouse (John L.

Kenney). Southampton—Lamont Smith; John Strong.
 Pennsylvania: Philadelphia—Charles Kline, University of Pennsylvania Museum Archives.
 Virginia: Richmond—Keith Egloff, Virginia Department of Historic Resources; William Rasmussen, Virginia Historical Society.
 Washington, D.C.—Joanna Scherer, Handbook Office, John Steiner, Photo Services, Vyrtis Thomas, National Anthropological Archives, Smithsonian Institution.

BIBLIOGRAPHY

BOOKS
Appelbaum, Diana Karter. *Thanksgiving: An American Holiday, an American History.* New York: Facts On File Publications, 1984.
Axtell, James. *The Invasion Within: The Contest of Cultures in Colonial North America.* New York: Oxford University Press, 1985.
Batkin, Jonathan, et al. *Eye of the Angel: Selections from the Derby Collection.* Ed. by David Wooley. Northampton, Massachusetts: White Star Press, 1990.
Beck, Horace P. *The American Indian as a Sea-Fighter in Colonial Times.* Mystic, Connecticut: The Marine Historical Association, 1959.
Bradford, William. *Of Plymouth Plantation, 1620-1647.* New York: Modern Library, 1981.
Burns, Rosemary H. *Mashpee, 1870-1995: 125th Anniversary.* Mashpee, Massachusetts: Town of Mashpee, 1995.
Calloway, Colin G. *The Abenaki.* New York: Chelsea House Publishers, 1989.
Calloway, Colin G., ed. and comp. *Dawnland Encounters: Indians and Europeans in Northern New England.* Hanover, New Hampshire: University Press of New England, 1991.
Clifford, James. *The Predicament of Culture: Twentieth-Century Ethnography, Literature, and Art.* Cambridge, Massachusetts: Harvard University Press, 1988.
Cronon, William. *Changes in the Land: Indians, Colonists, and the Ecology of New England.* New York: Hill and Wang, 1983.
Dial, Adolph L., and David K. Eliades. *The Only Land I Know: A History of the Lumbee Indians.* San Francisco: The Indian Historian Press, 1975.
Dowd, Gregory Evans. *The Indians of New Jersey.* Trenton: New Jersey Historical Commission, Department of State, 1992.
Feest, Christian F. *The Powhatan Tribes.* New York: Chelsea House Publishers, 1990.
Goodman, Jordan. *Tobacco in History: The Cultures of Dependence.* New York: Routledge, 1993.
Grumet, Robert S. *The Lenapes.* New York: Chelsea House Publishers, 1989.
Haviland, William A., and Marjory W. Power. *The Original Vermonters: Native Inhabitants, Past and Present.* Hanover, New Hampshire: University Press of New England, 1981.
Hulton, Paul. *America 1585: The Complete Drawings of John White.* Chapel Hill: University of North Carolina Press, 1984.
Kehoe, Alice Beck. *North American Indians: A Comprehensive Account.* Englewood Cliffs, New Jersey: Prentice-Hall, 1981.
Kraft, Herbert C. *The Lenape: Archaeology, History, and Ethnography.* Newark: New Jersey Historical Society, 1986.
Krech, Shepard, III, ed. *Passionate Hobby: Rudolf Frederick Haffenreffer and the King Philip Museum.* Bristol, Rhode Island: Haffenreffer Museum of Anthropology, Brown University, 1994.
Leland, Charles G. *The Algonquin Legends of New England.* Boston: Houghton, Mifflin, 1884.
Lester, Joan A.:
 History on Birchbark: The Art of Tomah Joseph, Passamaquoddy. Bristol, Rhode Island: Haffenreffer Museum of Anthropology, Brown University, 1993.
 We're Still Here: Art of Indian New England, The Children's Museum Collection. Boston: The Children's Museum, 1987.
Lewis, Thomas A. *For King and Country: The Maturing of George Washington, 1748-1760.* New York: HarperCollins, 1993.
Linton, Ralph. *Use of Tobacco among North American Indians.* Chicago: Field Museum of Natural History, 1924.
Little, Elizabeth A. *Indian Whalemen of Nantucket: The Documentary Evidence.* Nantucket, Massachusetts: Nantucket Historical Association, 1992.
Marten, Catherine. "The Wampanoags in the Seventeenth Century: An Ethnohistorical Survey." In *Occasional Papers in Old Colony Studies.* Plymouth, Massachusetts: Plimoth Plantation, 1970.
Mourt's relation. *A Relation . . . of the Beginning and Proceedings of the English Plantation Setled At Plimoth in New England.* Norwood, New Jersey: Walter J. Johnson, 1974 (reprint of 1622 edition).
Nash, Gary B. *Red, White, and Black: The Peoples of Early America.* Englewood Cliffs, New Jersey: Prentice-Hall, 1982.
Neustadt, Kathy. *Clambake: A History and Celebration of an American Tradition.* Amherst: University of Massachusetts Press, 1992.
New England Begins: The Seventeenth Century. Boston: Museum of Fine Arts, 1982.
Peters, Russell M. *Clambake: A Wampanoag Tradition.* Minneapolis: Lerner Publications, 1992.
Porter, Frank W. *The Nanticoke.* New York: Chelsea House Publishers, 1987.
Rasmussen, William M. S., and Robert S. Tilton. *Pocahontas: Her Life & Legend.* Richmond: Virginia Historical Society, 1994.
Rountree, Helen C.:
 Pocahontas's People: The Powhatan Indians of Virginia through Four Centuries. Norman: University of Oklahoma Press, 1990.
 The Powhatan Indians of Virginia: Their Traditional Culture. Norman: University of Oklahoma Press, 1989.
Rountree, Helen C., ed. *Powhatan: Foreign Relations, 1500-1722.* Charlottesville: University Press of Virginia, 1993.
Russell, Howard S. *Indian New England before the Mayflower.* Hanover, New Hampshire: University Press of New England, 1980.
Salisbury, Neal. *Manitou and Providence: Indians, Europeans, and the Making of New England, 1500-1643.* New York: Oxford University Press, 1982.
Sider, Gerald M. *Lumbee Indian Histories: Race, Ethnicity, and Indian Identity in the Southern United States.* New York: Cambridge University Press, 1993.
Simmons, William S. *Spirit of the New England Tribes: Indian History and Folklore, 1620-1984.* Hanover, New Hampshire: University Press of New England, 1986.
Speck, Frank G. *Penobscot Man: The Life History of a Forest Tribe in Maine.* New York: Octagon Books, 1970 (reprint of 1940 edition).
The Spirit Sings: Artistic Traditions of Canada's First Peoples. Toronto: McClelland and Stewart, 1987.
Stone, Gaynell, ed. *The Shinnecock Indians: A Culture History.* Riverhead, New York: Suffolk County Archaeological Association, 1983.
Strong, John A. "Indian Labor During the Post-Contact Period on Long Island, 1626-1700." In *To Know the Place: Exploring Long Island History.*

Ed. by Joann P. Krieg and Natalie A. Naylor. Interlaken, New York: Heart of the Lakes Publishing, 1995.

Tilton, Robert S. *Pocahontas: The Evolution of an American Narrative.* New York: Cambridge University Press, 1994.

Trigger, Bruce G., ed. *Northeast.* Vol. 15 of *Handbook of North American Indians.* Washington, D.C.: Smithsonian Institution, 1978.

Vaughan, Alden T. *New England Frontier: Puritans and Indians, 1620-1675.* Boston: Little, Brown, 1965.

Wallace, Paul A. W. *Indians in Pennsylvania.* Harrisburg: Pennsylvania Historical and Museum Commission, 1964.

Weslager, C. A.:
A Brief Account of the Indians of Delaware. Newark: University of Delaware Press, 1953.
The Delaware Indians: A History. New Brunswick, New Jersey: Rutgers University Press, 1972.

West, George A. *Tobacco, Pipes and Smoking Customs of the American Indians.* Westport, Connecticut: Greenwood Press, 1970 (reprint of 1934 edition).

Whitehead, Ruth Holmes. *Micmac Quillwork: Micmac Indian Techniques of Porcupine Quill Decoration, 1600-1950.* Halifax: Nova Scotia Museum, 1982.

Young, Alexander. *Chronicles of the Pilgrim Fathers of the Colony of Plymouth, from 1602 to 1625.* Boston: Charles C. Little and James Brown, 1841.

PERIODICALS
Bulletin of the Massachusetts Archaeological Society, October 1961.

Strong, John A.:
"The Reaffirmation of Tradition among the Native Americans of Eastern Long Island." *Long Island Historical Journal,* Fall 1994.
"Shinnecock and Montauk Whalemen." *The Long Island Historical Journal,* Fall 1989.

Vickers, Daniel:
"The First Whalemen of Nantucket." *William and Mary Quarterly,* 1983, Vol. 40.
"Nantucket Whalemen in the Deep-Sea Fishery: The Changing Anatomy of an Early American Labor Force." *The Journal of American History,* September 1985.

Yankee Magazine (New England Sampler section), May 1993.

OTHER SOURCES
Benes, Peter, ed. "Algonkians of New England: Past and Present." Report. Dublin Seminar for New England Folklife Annual Proceedings, June 29-30, 1991.

Pepper Bird Foundation. "American Indian Heritage and Cultural Interests." Pamphlet. Williamsburg, Virginia: Pepper Bird Publications, 1995.

PICTURE CREDITS

The sources for the illustrations that appear in this book are listed below. Credits from left to right are separated by semicolons; from top to bottom they are separated by dashes.

Cover: Historical Society of Pennsylvania, Philadelphia, no. 1834.3. **6, 7:** © Carr Clifton; University of Pennsylvania Museum, Philadelphia, neg. no. S4-141767. **8, 9:** © Paul O. Boisvert—Ogawinno Society, Odanak, courtesy Rick Obomsawin. **10, 11:** Justine Hill, Santa Monica, California; courtesy National Museum of the American Indian, Smithsonian Institution. **12, 13:** George Goodwin, Morristown, New Jersey; National Anthropological Archives (NAA), Smithsonian Institution, no. 56928. **14, 15:** Robert Kyle; NAA, Smithsonian Institution, no. 893. **16:** British Library, London. **18:** Mark Sexton, courtesy The Children's Museum, Boston. **19:** Map by Maryland CartoGraphics, Inc. **20, 21:** National Gallery of Canada, Ottawa, Ontario. **23:** © British Museum, London; University of Pennsylvania Museum, Philadelphia, neg. no. S4-1385. **24, 25:** The National Museum of Denmark, Department of Ethnography, photographer: Kit Weiss (2); courtesy Virginia Department of Historic Resources, photo by Katherine Wetzel—NAA, Smithsonian Institution, no. 4327; The National Museum of Denmark, Department of Ethnography, photographer: Kit Weiss. **27:** Courtesy Peabody Essex Museum, Salem, Massachusetts, neg. no. A3568. **28:** From *Penobscot Man*, by Frank G. Speck, University of Pennsylvania Press, 1940. **29:** Pitt Rivers Museum, Oxford, England. **30:** Waterloo Foundation for the Arts, Inc. **31:** University of Pennsylvania Museum, Philadelphia, neg. no. S35-13964. **32:** © Gale Zucker. **34:** Courtesy National Museum of the American Indian, Smithsonian Institution. **35:** The National Museum of Denmark, Department of Ethnography, photographer: Kit Weiss—courtesy National Museum of the American Indian, Smithsonian Institution. **36, 37:** © William B. Folsom. **38:** Courtesy of the Haffenreffer Museum of Anthropology, Brown University—courtesy of Plimoth Plantation, photograph by Gary Andrashko. **39:** Courtesy National Museum of the American Indian, Smithsonian Institution, no. 18/4443. **40:** University of Pennsylvania Museum, Philadelphia, neg. no. S4-13902. **42, 43:** © British Museum, London. **45:** New Brunswick Museum, Saint John. **46, 47:** © British Museum, London; Fil Hunter, courtesy Indian Village, Jamestown Settlement, Virginia (2). **48:** The National Museum of Denmark, Department of Ethnography, photographer: Kit Weiss. **51:** British Library, London. **52:** Courtesy National Museum of the American Indian, Smithsonian Institution, no. 2/814. **53:** Waterloo Foundation for the Arts, Inc. **54:** Courtesy Peabody Essex Museum, Salem, Massachusetts; Mark Sexton, courtesy The Children's Museum, Boston. **55:** Courtesy of the Haffenreffer Museum of Anthropology, Brown University. **56, 57:** Mark Sexton, courtesy The Children's Museum, Boston, except bottom right, Mark Sexton, courtesy Charles Adams. **58, 59:** Mark Sexton, courtesy James Richardson III; Mark Sexton, courtesy The Children's Museum, Boston (3). **60, 61:** Peabody Museum, Harvard University, no. N27296—from the collection of the Abbe Museum, Bar Harbor, Maine, photo by Stephen Bicknell; Mark Sexton, courtesy The Children's Museum, Boston—Thaw Collection, Fenimore House Museum, Cooperstown, New York (#T43), photographer: John Bigelow Taylor. **62:** NAA, Smithsonian Institution, no. 74-8367; Mark Sexton, courtesy The Children's Museum, Boston. **63:** Mark Sexton, courtesy The Children's Museum, Boston—*The Ellsworth American*, Ellsworth, Maine. **64:** Library of The Boston Atheneum. **66:** Courtesy of the John Carter Brown Library at Brown University. **67:** Plimoth Plantation. **68, 69:** © British Museum, London. **70:** Courtesy Virginia Department of Historic Resources, photo by Katherine Wetzel—courtesy of the Massachusetts Historical Society. **73:** © British Museum, London—Virginia Historical Society. **74:** The Museum of the Confederacy, Richmond, Virginia, photo by Katherine Wetzel—Virginia Historical Society (2). **75:** Kendall Whaling Museum, Sharon, Massachusetts; courtesy the Archives of the American Illustrators Gallery, New York, Howard Chandler Christy "Pocahontas," 1911. **76, 77:** Cook Collection, Valentine Museum, Richmond, Virginia. **78:** Collection of The New York Historical Society. **79:** Prints Division, The New York Public Library, Astor, Lenox and Tilden Foundations. **82, 83:** Murv Jacob, Tahlequah, Oklahoma. **84:** The Henry Huntington Library and Art Gallery, San Marino, California; Massachusetts Historical Society. **86:** Rhode Island Historical Society, RHi X3 2035. **87:** Courtesy American Antiquarian Society, Worcester, Massachusetts. **88:** M. J. Lopez, Mashpee, Massachusetts. **90, 91:** Gilcrease Institute of Art, Tulsa, Oklahoma; courtesy of National Museum of the American Indian, Smithsonian Institution, no. 5/3150. **92:** Chicago Historical Society, ICHi-08785. **93:** Courtesy American Antiquarian Society, Worcester, Massachusetts. **94, 95:** Bibliothèque Nationale de France, Paris. **97:** Library of Congress, Rare Books Division, Washington, D.C.; from the collection of the Abbe Museum, Bar Harbor, Maine, photos by Stephen Bicknell. **98:** Courtesy the Town of Southampton, New York, photo by Ron Papageorge. **99:** East Hampton Library, Long Island Collection, no. CH58—Old Dartmouth Historical Society, New Bedford Whaling Museum. **101:** © British Museum, London. **102, 103:** Ville de Montreal—Provincial Archives of New Brunswick, Taylor Col-

INDEX

Numerals in italics indicate an illustration of the subject mentioned.

A

Abenaki Indians: captives, 48; Europeans and, 68; French culture, influence of, *102*; fur trade, 96, 100; Iroquois and, 100; longhouses, 34; manitous, 48-49; marriage, 39; missionaries and, 102, 135; respect for animals, 49; seasonal farming, 33; snaring fish technique, *23. See also* Eastern Abenaki Indians; Penobscot Indians; Western Abenaki Indians
Abolitionists: 139, 140
Absentee Delawares: 124
Accomac Indians: antidiscrimination policy of, 144-145
Adams, Gideon (Narragansett Indian): quoted, 141
Adultery: 42
African slaves: 94
Ahsoo (Mashpee legend): 22
Alcohol: bribes, 87, *93*, 100, 139; renunciation, 130
Algonquian Indians: *70*; birch-bark container, *18*; early village, *16*; gender-specific chores, 36-38;

Gluskab legend, 17-18, 30, 53, 56, 57; migrations, 18-19; subsistence pattern diversity, 19-22; tree usage, 27-28; tribal homelands, *map* 19; wild plants, 29. *See also* specific tribes
American Revolution: 104; Delaware Indians and, 126-128; Penobscot, Passamaquoddy and, 134
Anderson, William (Delaware Indian): 131; quoted, 132
Anishinabe ("original people"): Ojibwa as, 18
Apess, William (Pequot Indian): quoted, 140
Appanaug (Mashpee Wampanoag Indian feast): 160, *160-169*
Arapaho Indians: 19
Arnold, Benedict: 134
Art: adorned clothing, *125, 130, 147-151;* Algonquian village engraving, *16;* birch-bark designs (Passamaquoddy), *18, 54-63, 152;* bowls, *38-39;* of Edward Hicks, *90-91;* of George Catlin, *122;* of John White, *42-43, 46, 68, 69, 73;* maps, *66, 68, 99;* Micmac village painting, *20-21;* of Murv Jacob, *82-83;* New Amsterdam painting, *79;* pipes, *114-117, 120-121;* Pocahontas images, *73-75;* quillwork designs

(Micmac), *105-111;* of Tomah Joseph, *54-63;* wampum beads, belts, *45, 91*
Attean, John (Penobscot Indian): 135, 136
Attean, Joseph (Penobscot Indian): 136
Audubon, John James: 132

B

Basket trap (Nanticoke): *25*
Beate (Delaware prophet): 129
Bess, Henry (Thunder Bird; Shinnecock Indian): 112
Beverley, Robert: quoted, 92, 100
Bible translation: 84, 85
Big House Ceremony (Lenape, Delaware): 51, 128, 129
Bingo gambling: 156-157, *158-159*
Birch-bark designs (Passamaquoddy): *18, 54-63, 152*
Birthing huts: 35
Blackfeet Indians: 19
Black William (Algonquian Indian): 64
Bourne, Richard: 88
Bradford, William: on Chief Massasoit, 66; on Indian hostility, 65; on Plymouth epidemic, 80; on Tisquantum, 67
Brothertown, New York: 101-102, 140

Brown, William (Delaware Indian): *117*
Buckskin coat (Delaware): *130*

C

Canoe building: birch-bark model, *60-61;* materials of, 25; Penobscot, *27;* Powhatan, 38
Canonchet (Narragansett Indian): 87, 89
Canonicus (Narragansett Indian): 81
Carter, Joey (Pequot Indian): *159*
Carver, John: *116*
Catlin, George: painting by, *123*
Cautantowwit (Narragansett creator): 48, 50-51
Ceremonies. *See* Rituals, ceremonies
Champlain, Samuel de: 65
Charlestown reservation, Rhode Island: 140
Cheepi (Narragansett deity): 49
Cherokee Indians: 132-133
Cheyenne Indians: 19
Children: mothers and, *20, 36, 40;* punishment, 42
Christianity. *See* Cultural assimilation; Missionaries
Christy, Howard Chandler: painting by, *75*
Citizenship: 155

Civil War: Delawares in, 132; Powhatans in, 146
Clan organization: 42
Clark, Charles C., IV (Nanticoke Indian): *120-121;* quoted, 121
Clark, Lydia (Nanticoke Indian): 142
Clothing: European influences on, *147-151*
Cochenoe (Massachusett Indian): 84
Colonists: in Connecticut, Massachusetts, 80-81, 84-89; first Thanksgiving, *82-83;* fur trade, 77, 78, 79, 80, 96; King Philip's War, 87-89, 104; Maryland colonization, 76-77; in New Amsterdam, New York, 77-80; in Pennsylvania, 89, 91; slavery, servants, 92-94; Virginia colonization, 68-76; whaling, 92, *97-99,* map, *99. See also* Missionaries
Confederacy, the: currency, *74*
Corn: Green corn festival (Algonquian), *46, 47;* importance of, 33; preparation of, *34-35, 43*
Coshocton (Delaware village): 127
Council house: 35
Courtship rituals: 41
Creation legends: Gluskab, 17-18, 30; Great Hare (Powhatan), 6, 19, 50, 53; Lenape, 51; Maushop (Wampanoag), 11, 53
Cuffe, Paul (Wampanoag Indian): 139, *140*
Cuffee, Warren (Shinnecock Indian): *142*
Cultural assimilation: clothing, *147-151;* European goods, 94-95; fur trade, 96, 100; land sale, 100-101; missionaries, 101-104; spiritual traditions, 85-86, 103. *See also* Missionaries; Racial discrimination; *and specific tribes*
Cultural preservation: Mashpee Wampanoag Indian feast, *160-169;* pan-Indian movement, 154-155; Penobscots, 152-154; Powhatans, 146, 154-155

D
Dale, Thomas: 72
Dean, Nora Thompson (Delaware Indian): *119*
Delaware Indian Resource Center: Ward Pound Ridge Reservation, New York, *119*
Delaware Indians: and American Revolution, 126-128; Big House Ceremony, 51, 128, 129; buckskin coat, *130;* Civil War, 132; French and Indian War, 123-126; herbalist, *119;* Lenape known as, 12, 21, 112, 123; missionaries and, *131;* Nonondagumun, *122;* Oklahoma log farmhouse, *132-133;* pipe tomahawk, *117;* relocation to Kansas, 131-132; relocation to Oklahoma, *map* 124, 132-133; silver treaty pipe, *127;* War of 1812, 130-131.

See also Lenape Indians
Denis, Joseph Paul (Western Abenaki Indian): *152*
Denton, Daniel: quoted, 79-80
Discrimination. *See* Racial discrimination
Diseases: from Europeans, 65, 66, 68, 71, 72, 77, 85, 104; smallpox, *92,* 104
Don Luis (Algonquian Indian): 68-69
Dutch: fur trade, 77, 78, 79; land claimed by, *94-95;* New Amsterdam, 77-80

E
Eastern Abenaki Indians: *map* 19; colonists and, 87; meals, 28; sacred Mount Katahdin, *6-7,* 49; Verrazano and, 68. *See also* Penobscot Indians
Education: Penobscots, 157; in praying towns, 86
Elders, caring for: 42
Eliot, John: *84,* 85, 86

F
Fallen Timbers, Battle of (1794): 129
Farming: northern New England, 19; seasonal nature, 33; southern New England, Middle Atlantic, 21-22
Father Sam (Samuel Niles): 101-102
Figurehead, ship's: Pocahontas as, *75*
Fire: usage of, 35
Fishing economy: ice fishing, 24; maritime resources, 22-25, *24-25;* spawning run fishing, 22
Food: 28-29; corn preparation, *34-35, 43;* hominy meal, *42-43;* Mashpee Wampanoag Indian feast, *160-169*
Fort Duquesne: 125
Fort Pitt: 126
Foxwoods (casino), Connecticut: *158-159*
Freewill Baptist church: 102
Frémont, John: 132
French and Indian War (1754-1763): 123-126, 134
Fur trade: Delaware, 126; Dutch, 77, 78, 79; French, 80; impact of, 96, 100

G
Gardiners Island, Long Island, New York: map, *99*
Gay Head, Martha's Vineyard, Massachusetts: *10-11*
Gay Head Wampanoag: 155, 157
Gingaskins (Accomacs): 144-145
Gluskab (Penobscot legend): 17-18, 30, 53, 56, 57
Gnadenhutten (Delaware village): 128
Great Awakening: 101-102
Great Hare (Powhatan creation legend): 6, 19, 50, 53
Green corn festival (Algonquian): *46, 47*

Gunpowder flask (Penobscot): *136-137*

H
Hackensack Lenape Indians: 78-79
Hanson, Elizabeth: quoted, 28
Harman, Isaac (Nanticoke Indian): 142-143
Harness racing: *74*
Harriot, Thomas: quoted, 43
Harrison, William Henry: Delaware treaties, 127; War of 1812, 131
Haskins, Amos (Wampanoag Indian): *99*
Hayward, Richard "Skip" (Pequot Indian): 157-158
Hendricks, Ralph (Wampanoag Indian): *163*
Hesselius, Gustavus: painting by, *cover*
Hicks, Edward: painting by, *90-91*
Hill, Tom (Poospatuck Indian): *24-25*
Hobomock (Wampanoag Indian): 67
Honorable, Dorcas (Wampanoag Indian): *143*
Hospitality customs (Lenape): 26
Hudson, Henry: 77
Hunting: birch-bark scenes, *58-59;* Lenapes, 30; Micmacs, 23-24, 30, 31; moose hunting, *28,* 152-153; Penobscots, *28, 31,* 152-153; respect for animals, 49; taboos, 49
Hunt, Thomas: 65
Huskanaw (puberty ritual): 39, 41

I
Indentured servants: 93
Indian Council of New England: 154
Indian Trade and Intercourse Act (1790): 155
Iopassus (Powhatan Indian): 50
Iroquois Indians: Algonquian name, 28; attack by, 35, 76-77, 100; French and Indian War, 123-124; fur trade, 100; Lenape domination, 123-124; location of, 19; longhouses, 34; Nanticokes and, 94; Wabanaki and, 134. *See also* Oneida Indians

J
Jacob, Murv: painting by, *82-83*
James I, King (England): 71
Jamestown: 71-72
Jesuit missionaries: 68-70, 135
Johnson, Fielding: quoted, 132
Joseph, Sabattis (Passamaquoddy Indian): *62;* wastebasket made by, *62*
Joseph, Tomah (Passamaquoddy Indian): *54, 58, 60;* canoe made by, *153;* continuing the tradition of, *62-63;* family gathering, *63;* hunting scenes, *58-59;* mythological characters, *56-57;* owl image used by, *54;* two-tiered picnic basket, *55;* waterway scenes, *60-61*

K
Kalm, Pehr: 28; quoted, 29
Kenney, John (Shinnecock Indian): 119
King Philip's War: 83, 86, 87-89, 104
Kinnikinnick (tobacco mixture): 112
Kiwasa (Roanoke deity): 51

L
Lake Champlain (New York-Vermont border): *8-9*
Land loss: Lenapes, 91; Mashpees, 140; Nanticokes, 77; Narragansetts, 141; Niantics, 100-101; Passamaquoddies, 134; Penobscots, 134, 135, 137; Wabanakis, 135; Wampanoags, 87, 137
Land restitution: 155; Mashpee Wampanoags, 157; Oneidas, 155; Penobscots, 156-157; Pequots, 157-158
Lapowinsa (Lenape Indian): *cover*
Lawson, John: quoted, 26
Legends: birch-bark mythological characters, *56-57;* Cautantowwit (Narragansett creation), 48; Cheepi (Narragansett deity), 49; creation, 17-18, 30, 51, 52; Dawnland, *6-7,* 18; farming, 33; Gluskab (Penobscot), 17-18, 30, 53, 56, 57; Great Hare (Powhatan), 6, 19, 50, 53; Kiwasa (Roanoke deity), 51; Maushop creation (Wampanoag), 11, 53; Mesingw (Lenape Keeper of Game), *52,* 53, *114, 128, 129;* Okeus (Powhatan deity), 48, *51;* People of the Dawnland, *6-7,* 18; Pomola (Abenaki), 49; sacred Mount Katahdin, *6-7,* 49; Skatekamuc (Micmac), 49; spirits, 49; Trout Chief, 22
Leland, Charles: 54
Lenape Indians: *map* 19; autumn rite, 51; children, 42; colonists and, 77-80, *79,* 89, 91; courtship rituals, 41; creation legend, 51; Delaware name, 12, 21, 112, 123; European clothing, 96; fur trade, 96; gender status, 39; hospitality customs, 26; hunting, 30, 49; Iroquois domination, 123-124; longhouses, 34, 51; medicine, 30; Mesingw (Keeper of Game) legend, *52,* 53, *114, 128, 129;* missionaries and, 103, 125; mother and daughter, *13;* mourning, 50; Munsee tribal branch, 12; New Amsterdam sale, 78; pipe bowl, *112;* prophet, 104; puberty rituals, 39; Quakers, 89; spawning fishing, 22; spirits after death, 49-50; subsistence pattern, 21; tobacco pipes, *115;* tobacco pouch, *113;* travel expertise, 26; tribal leadership, 44; Verrazano and, 67; Walking Purchase, 91, 123; war club, *48;* war parties, 48; wigwam, *30;* William Penn and, 89, *90-91. See also*

Delaware Indians
Lindestrom, Peter: 115
Lobster net (Wampanoag): *24*
Long-handled spear (Abenaki): *23*
Longhouses: 34, 51

M

McCullough, John: quoted, 49
Mahican Indians: Henry Hudson and, 77; Lenapes and, 79; longhouses, 34; missionaries and, 102-103; spawning fishing, 22; subsistence pattern, 21; wampum, 96
Maine Woods, The (Thoreau): 136
Maliseet Indians: *map* 19; agriculture of, 19; Christianity, conversion to, *102-103*; clothing, 147; courtship rituals, 41; handcrafted wares, *138*
Mamanatowick (Powhatan paramount chief): 45
Manitous (spirits): 48-53; Abenaki, 49; appeasement of, 49; burying the dead, 50; ceremonies, 50-51; creation legends, 51-53; after death, 49-50; of Narragansetts, 48; Powhatan spirits after death, 50; of Wampanoag, 49. *See also* Legends
Marriage: 39, 41-42
Marshall, Edward: 91
Martha's Vineyard, Massachusetts: *10-11*
Maryland colonization: 76-77
Mashpee Indians: land loss, 140; land restitution, 157; Mashpee Revolt, 140; refuge to groups, 139; Richard Bourne and, *88*; self-rule petition, 137, 139; spawning run fishing, 22. *See also* Mashpee Wampanoag Indian feast
Mashpee Wampanoag Indian feast: bake pit, *160-161*; baking, tale-telling, *166-167*; gathering ingredients, *162-163*; origin of, 160; sharing the bounty, *168-169*; stoking the oven, *164-165*
Massachuset Indians: *84, 85*; migratory life, 21
Massachusetts Bay Colony: 84; land purchased by, 80; Roger Williams and, 81; seal, *76*; Wampanoags and, 139
Massasoit (Wampanoag Indian): first Thanksgiving and, 82; Plymouth colonists and, 65-66, 81, *116*; son Metacomet, 87
Massasoit (whaling vessel): 99
Matoaka (Pocahontas): 73
Mattaponi Indians: cultural preservation, 146; gambling casinos, 159; Powhatan Confederacy, 154
Maushop (Wampanoag creation legend): 11, 53
Mauwee, Eunice (Pequot Indian): *144*
Medicine: 29-30
Melville, Herman: 135
Menstrual huts: 35, 39, 86

Mesingw (Lenape Keeper of Game legend): *52, 53, 114, 128, 129*
Metacomet (Wampanoag Indian): 87
Miami Indians: Delaware alliance, 129; War of 1812, 131
Miantonomi (Narragansett Indian): 81, 84; quoted, 85
Micmac Indians: *map* 19, *20-21, 144*; clothing, 147, *148*; Europeans and, 68; fur trade, 96; hunting, 23-24, 30, 31; medicine, 30; moose caller, *29*; peaked cap, *147*; pipe, *116*; quillwork, *105-111*; Skatekamuc deity, 49; smoking bag, *117*; tobacco cultivation, 19; tribal leadership, 44; wampum beads, *45*; wigwam, 30, 33
Mikamwes (woods dweller; Passamaquoddy legend): 57, 63
Minisink Island: 12
Minuit, Peter: 78
Miquon (William Penn): 90
Missionaries: Great Awakening, 101-102; Jesuits, 68-70, 135; among Mahicans, 102-103; among Mashpees, *88*; Massachusetts Bay Colony, 84; Moravian Church, 103, 126, 129; Natick praying town, 85-86; Oklahoma Delaware as, *131*; among Powhatans, 103-104; Sebastian Rasles, *135*; among Wabanakis, 102
Moby Dick (Melville): 136
Mohawk Indians: English and, 86
Mohegan Indians: colonists and, 88; migratory life, 21; Narragansett and, 84; wooden bowl, 84
Montauk Indians: *map* 19; colonists and, 84-85; shell wampum strings, 23; whaling, 97
Month of Smelts (Spearfish Moon; April): 22, 23
Moose caller (Micmac): *29*
Moose hunting (Penobscot): *28,* 152-153
Moravian Church: 103, 126, 129
Morris, Christina (Micmac Indian): *147*
Mortar and pestle: corn processed with, *34-35*
Mount Katahdin, Maine: *6-7,* 49
Munimkwes (Woodchuck; Passamaquoddy legend): 57
Munsee Indians: 12
Murphy, Joe (Passamaquoddy Indian): box made by, *63*

N

Nada'buna (Carrying the Bed; Penobscot ritual): 41
Nanticoke Indians: *map* 19; basket trap, *25*; burial, 50; colonists and, 77, 94; corn preparation, *34*; cultural preservation, 143-144; discrimination against, 141-144; pipe ceremony, *120-121*; Piscataway similarity, 36; Powwow, *156-157*;

subsistence pattern, 21, 33; tribal leadership, 44
Narragansett Indians: *map* 19; assimilation, 136; Cautantowwit legend, 48, 50-51; Cheepi deity, 49; Christianity and, 101-102; colonists and, 80-81, 84-85, *86,* 87, 92; cultural preservation, 154; interracial marriages, 139-140; King Philip's War, 89, 104; land loss, 140-141; land restitution, 155; manitous, 46, 47; migratory life, 21; Mohegans and, 84; polygamy, 41; seasonal festivities, 35-36; stonemasonry, 137; tribal leadership, 44; Verrazano and, 67; Wampanoag and, 66, 81
Natick, Massachusetts (praying town): 86
Neolin (Lenape Indian): 126; quoted, 104
Nepinough (Earing of the Corn) season: 33
Netawatwees (Wyandot Indian): 126
Netting needle (Pamunkey): *24*
New Amsterdam: *79*; coat of arms, *78*; fur trade center, 78
Newcomerstown, Ohio: 126
Newell, Irene (Passamaquoddy Indian): basket made by, *139*
New Lights: 102
New York (New Amsterdam): 79
Niantic Indians: clothing, *149*; Narragansett and, 89; Pequot control of, 81; tribal lands, 100-101. *See also* Narragansett Indians
Nicholas, Louis (Penobscot Indian): 153
Nicola, Peter (Penobscot Indian): *150*
Nicotiana rustica: 112, 113
Niles, Samuel (Narragansett Indian): 101-102
Ninigret, George (Niantic Indian): 101
Ninigret, Thomas (Niantic Indian): 101
Ninigret II (Niantic Indian): 100-101
Nipmuck Indians: *map* 19; colonists and, 87; migratory life, 21; Seaquankeyquash ceremony, *32*; wooden bowl, *38*
Noka, Joshua H. (Narragansett Indian): quoted, 141
Nonondagumun (Delaware Indian): *122*
Nonsuch, Mercy (Niantic Indian): *149*

O

Odzihoso (Western Abenaki transformer): 9
Ojibwa Indians: as Anishinabe ("original people"), 18
Okeus (Powhatan deity): 48, *51*
Oneida Indians: land restitution, 155; Narragansett and, 140
Opechancanough (Powhatan Indian): 72, 76

Orono, Joseph (Penobscot Indian): 136
Osage Indians: Delaware Indians and, 132
Ossuary (common grave): 50
Ottawa Indians: Chief Pontiac, 126

P

Pamunkey Indian Reservation, Virginia: 14
Pamunkey Indians: ceremonial regalia, *15*; cultural preservation, 154; deer tribute, *154*; discrimination against, 146; family portrait, *145*; gambling, 159; John Smith rescue performance, *76-77*; land restitution, 155; netting needle, *24*
Pamunkey River: *14-15*
Pan-Indian movement: 154-155
Passamaquoddy Indians: *142*; birch-bark designs, *18, 54-63*; clothing, 147; land loss, 134; land restitution, 155-156; Tomah Joseph, 54-63, *54, 58, 60,* 153; woven basket, *139. See also* Maliseet Indians
Patawomeck Indians: 72
Paul, Gabe (Penobscot Indian): 151
Penn, Thomas: 91
Penn, William: Indian rights policy, 89; on Lenape chiefs, 44; Lenape peace treaty, 90-91
Penobscot Indians: boatman, *137*; chief in regalia, *7*; clan organization, 42; clothing, 147, *148, 150, 151*; cultural preservation, 152-154; father and son hunting, *31*; guides, 136; gunpowder flask, *136-137*; land loss, 134, 135, 137; land restitution, 155, 156-157; Louis Sockalexis, *143,* 156, 157; marriage rituals, 41; medicine, 30; missionaries and, 102; moose hunting, *28,* 152-153; mother rocking baby, *40*; sacred Mount Katahdin, *6-7,* 49; spawning fishing, 22; venture capital from, 158; village, *27*
Pequot Indians: *map* 19; antidiscrimination policy of, 140; assimilation, 136; bingo, casino, 158-159; colonists and, 81; cultural preservation, 154, 157-158; Eunice Mauwee, *144*; land restitution, 155, 157-158; migratory life, 21; Narragansett and, 81; wampum, 96; whaling, 137
Peters, Russell (Mashpee Wampanoag Indian): *160, 162, 164-165, 168*
Pilgrims: first Thanksgiving, *82-83*; John Carver, *116*; Plymouth harbor, 66
Pipes: *114-117, 120-121*
Pipe tomahawk: *101, 116-117*
Piscataway Indians: *map* 19; clay bowls, *37*; colonists and, 76-77; subsistence pattern, 21; tribal leadership, 44; village replica, *36*

Plains Indians: Delaware clothing style, *130;* pan-Indian community, *156-157*
Pleasant Point Reservation: 155-156
Plimoth Plantation, Massachusetts: 67
Plouffe, Elizabeth George (Pequot Indian): quoted, 157
Plymouth colony: first Thanksgiving, *82-83;* Wampanoags, 81
Plymouth harbor: map, *66*
Pocahontas: abduction, marriage, 45, 72; descendants, 146; images of, *73-75;* John Smith legend, 45, 71
Polygamy: Narragansetts, 41; Powhatans, 41-42, 45; prohibition of, 86
Pomola (Abenaki spirit): 49
Pontiac (Ottawa Indian): 126
Poospatuck Indians: *24-25*
Port Saint Louis (Plymouth harbor): map, *66*
Powhatan, Chief: colonists and, 71-72; multitribal chiefdom, 14, 21-22, 68; Pocahontas, John Smith legend, 45-46; quoted, 72
Powhatan Confederacy: 154-155
Powhatan Guards (Company E, Virginia Cavalry): banner, *74*
Powhatan Indians: *map 19;* alcohol, 100; canoe building, 38; colonists and, 72, 76, 92; cultural preservation, 154-155, 159; discrimination against, 144-145, 146; Great Hare creation legend, 6, 19, 50, 53; James Revell, 93-94; missionaries and, 103-104; Okeus deity, 51; Pocahontas, 45, 71-72, *73-75;* polygamy, 41; puberty rituals, 39, 41; as slaves, 93; spawning fishing, 22; spirits after death, 50; subsistence pattern, 21, 33; trade, 25-26; tribal leadership, 44, 45-46; walnut milk, 28. *See also* Mattaponi Indians; Pamunkey Indians
Praying towns: 85-86, 88
Premarital sex: 41
Puberty rituals: 30, 41
Puccoon (red root powder): 25
Puritans: diseases, 65, 80; praying towns, 86; Tisquantum and, 65-67. *See also* Plymouth colony

Q
Quakers: 89
Quillwork designs (Micmac): *105-111*

R
Racial discrimination: by Algonquians, 139-140; civil rights, 155; laws passed, 145-146; against Nanticoke Indians, 141-144; against Powhatans, 144-145, 146; against southern Algonquians, 141-146
Racial Integrity Law (1924): 146
Rasles, Sebastian: *135*
Reconstruction, Powhatans in: 146

Revell, James (Powhatan Indian): 93-94
Revolutionary War. *See* American Revolution
Rituals, ceremonies: autumn, harvest, 50-51; Big House Ceremony (Lenape, Delaware), 51, 128, 129; courtship, marriage, 41; Green corn festival (Algonquian), *46, 47;* pipes, *114-117;* puberty, 39, 41; reaffirming old ways, *118-119;* Seaquankeyquash (Nipmuck spring ceremony), *32;* tobacco ceremony, *112-113, 120-121*
Roanoke Indians: *map 19;* colonists and, 69; Europeans and, 70-71; Kiwasa deity, 51; land reverence, 17; subsistence pattern, 21
Robb, Charles: *154*
Robert Abbe Museum: 63
Rolfe, John: Pocahontas marriage to, 45, 72, 73, 146
Roosevelt, Franklin Delano: *153*

S
Sachems (chiefs): 44
Sagamore (Micmac tribal leader): 44
Saint Marys, Maryland: 76
Seaquankeyquash (Nipmuck spring ceremony): *32*
Seasons passing: Abenaki farming, 33; corn importance, 33; festivities, 35-36; Micmac hunting, 31; Nipmuck spring ceremony, *32*
Secotan Indians: *69*
Sergeant, John: 103
Shackamaxon: *90-91*
Shawnee Indians: Delaware alliance, 129; Tenskwatawa (prophet), 129-130
Shelters: of Micmacs, 33; multifamily longhouses, 34; village location, 34-35; year-round shelters, 33-34. *See also* Wigwams
Shingas (Lenape Indian): 123-124, 126
Shinnecock Indians: Civil War veteran, *142;* shell wampum strings, 23; tobacco plant, *118;* tobacco pouch, *119;* tobacco ritual, 112; whaling, 97, 98
Shinnecock Reservation, Long Island, New York: 118
Skatekamuc (Micmac deity): 49
Slany, John: 65
Slavery: of Indians, 92-94
Smallpox: *92,* 104
Smith, John: 71-72, 73; quoted, 45
Smith, Lamont (Shinnecock Indian): *118*
Smoking bag: *117*
Sockalexis, Louis (Penobscot Indian): *143,* 156, 157
Sockum, Levin (Nanticoke Indian): 142-143
Spanish Jesuits: 68-70
Spearfish Moon (Month of Smelts; April): 22, 23

Speck, Frank: quoted, 152-154
Spelman, Henry: 50
Spiritual traditions: Big House Ceremony (Delaware), 129; loss of, 85, 103. *See also* Rituals, ceremonies
Squanto (Tisquantum; Wampanoag Indian): 65-67
Stafford, Emma M. (Wampanoag Indian): *11*
Susquehannock Indians: 76-77
Sweat lodges: 35

T
Taboos, hunting: 49
Tecumseh (Shawnee Indian): 130
Tenskwatawa (Shawnee Indian): 129-130
Thanksgiving, first: *82-83*
Thoreau, Henry David: 136
Thunder Bird (Henry Bess; Shinnecock Indian): 112
Tidewater Virginia: 14
Tishcohan (Lenape Indian): *113*
Tisquantum (Squanto; Wampanoag Indian): 65-67
Tobacco: *118;* ceremonial ritual, *112-113, 120-121;* cultural preservation, *118-119;* pipes, *114-117, 120-121;* Powhatans and, 72, 76; significance, 112; tobacco pouch, *119. See also* Rituals, ceremonies
Tomahawk pipe: *101, 116-117*
Tomahawks: *101, 116-117*
Tourist trade: birch-bark designs, *54-55;* Pequots, 137; Wabanakis, 135
Trade: 25-26
Travel: Indian expertise, customs, 26-27
Tribal homelands: *map 19*
Tribal leadership: 44-45
Tribal warfare: 100
Trout Chief (Mashpee legend): 22
Tuckahoe roots: 29
Turner, Nat: 142, 145

U
United Colonies of New England: 85
Upper Delaware River: *12-13*

V
Van de Passe, Simon: 73
Verrazano, Giovanni da: 67-68
Villages: 34-35, *46-47*
Virginia Cavalry (Powhatan Guards): 74
Virginia colonization: 68-76

W
Wabanaki Indians: colonists and, 92; European clothing, 94, 96, 147; Europeans and, 68; French fur trade, 80; land loss, 135; lifestyle of, 19, 135; missionaries and, 102; People of the Dawnland, 18; relocation, 134. *See also* Abenaki Indians; Micmac Indians; Passamaquoddy Indians
Walking Purchase: 91, 123

Walnut milk: 28
Wampanoag Indians: *map 19;* assimilation, 136; Chief Massasoit, 65-66, 81, 82, 87, *116;* clay pot, *38;* colonists and, 65-67, 80-81, *82-83,* 87-89; Dorcas Honorable, *143;* Emma M. Stafford, *11;* epidemic, 65-66; King Philip's War, 87-89, 104; land loss, 87, 137; land restitution, 155; lobster net, *24;* missionaries and, 87; Maushop legend, 53; origin legend, 11; Paul Cuffe, *140;* peace pipe, *116;* spirits, 49; subsistence pattern of, 21; Tisquantum (Squanto), 65-67; travel customs, 26-27; tribal leadership, 44; whaling, 97, 99, 137, 139; wigwam, *67;* wooden ladle, *39. See also* Mashpee Indians; Mashpee Wampanoag Indian feast
Wampum: colonists and, 96; Lenape belt, *91;* Micmac beads, *45;* of shells, 23
War of 1812: 130-131
War chiefs: 48
War club (Lenape): *48*
Ward Pound Ridge Reservation, New York: *119*
Washington, George: 134
Waterloo Village, New Jersey: 30
Waterway birch-bark scenes: *60-61*
Wayne, Anthony "Mad": 129
Wequash (Algonquian Indian): 85
Werowance (Powhatan chief): 45
Western Abenaki Indians: *8, map 19;* agriculture of, 19; birch-bark canoe models, *152;* cattails, 29; clan organization, 42; tribal leadership, 44
Whale-bone arrowpoint: *97*
Whaling: 92, *97-99,* 137, 139
White, John: map by, *68;* watercolors by, *42-43, 46, 69, 73*
Wigwams: Algonquian, 33, *46-47;* Lenape, *30;* Wampanoag, *67*
Williams, Roger: on berries, 29; on community spirit, 35-36; on gender roles, 38; Indian rights policy, 85, 89; on Narragansett spirits, 48; Rhode Island, 81; on tribal warfare, 100; on Wampanoag spirits, 49
Wingina (Roanoke Indian): 71
Winslow, Edward: quoted, 38, 82
Wise Owl, Chief (Nipmuck Indian): *32*
Women: chores of, 36, 38-39; clothing decoration, 147; corn preparation, 33, *34;* hide preparation, 96; marriage, 39, 41-42; mourning, 50; puberty rituals, 39; quillwork designs, 105; sap collection, 28; status, 38-39; trading missions, 26
Wood, William: quoted, 24-25
World War II: 153
Wyandot Indians: 126

X
Xingwikaon (Delaware Big House): *128*